FOR JONATHAN AND CINDY

the little book of
CROPS
IN SMALL SPOTS

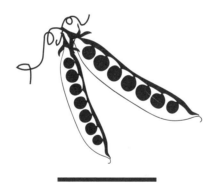

jane moore

photography by emli bendixen

Hardie Grant

QUADRILLE

CONTENTS

INTRODUCTION 4
GETTING STARTED 9
WHAT TO GROW YOUR
PLANTS IN 12
GET GROWING 16
PESTS AND DISEASES 22

WINDOW GROWING 26
MICRO-GREENS AND
CRESS 30
CHILLIES 33
PEA SHOOTS 36
WINDOWSILL TOMATOES 38
AUBERGINE OR EGGPLANT 41
HERBS AND SALADS 45

SMALL GARDENS 46
CARROTS 52
CHARD 54
CLIMBING OR POLE
BEANS 56
COMPANION PLANTING 59
POTATOES 63
SUMMER SALADS 65
BEETROOT OR BEET 69

SPACE SAVERS 70
MINI CABBAGES 74
STRAWBERRIES 77
MINI LETTUCES 80
RADISHES 83

SPRING ONIONS OR
    SCALLIONS 86
KOHL RABI 89

CROPS IN POTS 90
    TOMATOES 96
    FRUIT BUSHES 99
    FRUIT TREES 102
    BEANS 106
    CULINARY HERBS 109
    ROOTS IN POTS 113
    SALADS IN CONTAINERS 116
    COURGETTE OR
        ZUCCHINI 119
    EDIBLE FLOWERS 122

EXTEND THE SEASON 124
    GARLIC 129
    BROAD, FAVA OR
        FABA BEANS 131
    KALE 135

PUMPKIN AND
    SQUASHES 136
WINTER GREENS 139

EAT THE UNUSUAL 142
    CUCAMELONS 146
    ASPARAGUS PEAS 149
    TOMATILLO 151
    AMARANTH OR
        CALLALOO 152
    MUSHROOMS 155
    LEMONS 156

GARDENERS' DICTIONARY
158

ACKNOWLEDGEMENTS 160

INTRODUCTION

Growing your own fruit and vegetables is well within the reach of anyone, no matter how much gardening you've done before. We all have to start somewhere, usually with a tomato plant, and that isn't the easiest crop to grow by any means. Begin by trying to grow a few different plants - you'll soon gain some confidence and knowledge, and then you'll be ready to branch out into other crops.

Simple, straightforward crops such as salad leaves, herbs and even a pot of home-grown cress can add so much to your meals and they are super easy to grow. Once you've mastered these, you'll feel ready to broaden your scope, expanding production and trying your hand at the more demanding crops.

Use your space wisely and even the smallest or most awkward spots can be brilliantly productive and a joy to own. Look at the colourful flowers on your vegetable plants and the bees that visit them, listen to the birdsong as they flit about snatching the insects that your plants have attracted and watch those fruits and pods swell with promise.

A FEW ESSENTIALS

- The growing instructions and suggestions are based firmly in the northern hemisphere. Many of these crops can be grown throughout the world, but you may need to adjust timings and care according to your seasons and how mild or extreme they are.

- Variety notes are just suggestions - there may be plant varieties that are far better suited to your climate than those I have listed. There are

hundreds of different vegetables and fruits out there – more than I could ever grow in a lifetime of gardening. So take advice locally from garden centres and nurseries. Of course, fellow gardeners are the best source of tips, tricks and top varieties, and are usually very happy to share their wisdom.

- Use the information on the seed packet. These are your instructions on when to sow, how deep and what conditions the plants will need to thrive. Planting depth is crucial – plant too deep and the seedlings will struggle to get to the surface, too shallow and the wind will blow them away or the birds will have them.

- The Gardeners' Dictionary on pages 158-59 provides useful explanations of any gardening phrases I have used, so do refer to this if needed.

HOW MUCH SUN?

Most vegetables need sunshine to thrive but awkward spots are not always that great for allowing in plenty of sun, especially between buildings where the walls can shade for much of the day. A lot of crops need full sun, which is around eight or more hours a day, or partial sun, which is about four hours or so.

As a rule of thumb, crops such as tomatoes, apples, pumpkins and courgettes/zucchini need plenty of sunshine to fully ripen, so give these your sunniest spots. Leafy crops such as beans, lettuces and salads generally will tolerate more shade.

HOW MUCH WATER?

Don't underestimate how much water even a single plant will demand throughout a season of growing. These plants grow fast and furious and you need to keep up with them if you're going to get the best results.

KEY TO SYMBOLS

◐ Plant spring, summer, autumn, winter

❀ Harvest spring, summer, autumn, winter

📅 Weeks to harvest

🪴 Skill level easy/ intermediate/challenging

☀ sunlight

🪣 watering

↑↑ height

✻ flower

seeds

feed

If you're growing in the ground, in a raised bed or something similar, then the natural supplies available from rainfall will help, although you will still need to supplement this. But I suspect that, like me, you'll be growing many of your crops in containers and these are totally reliant on you for providing water and nutrients, as rain will barely penetrate a pot as the compost surface will be covered by the foliage of the plant. Plants growing in pots and containers (including grow bags) will need watering sometimes daily throughout the growing season, so plan ahead, setting up water butts and containers to catch rainfall where possible. An automatic watering system makes life easier and, if it has a timer, it means you can water at night when the plant is able to make the most of the precious water without it evaporating in the heat of the day.

GETTING STARTED

It doesn't matter how small a space you have or how inexperienced you are, growing your own crops in spare corners of your garden or on a patio is easy to do. In a way, growing in odd spots is ideal for developing your gardening skills as it forces you to start small, mastering one or two crops before you move on to more varied plants that require more management.

When we met, my partner had started his gardening life with a single tomato plant on the windowsill of his fourth floor flat. After a couple of seasons, he had progressed to several pots of herbs, a couple of tomato plants and a tub or two of potatoes. By then he had run out of space, and that's the tricky thing with odd-spot growing - there just isn't enough room for everything you want to grow. You can't go wrong if you choose the crops you love to have at hand, the ones you want to eat freshly picked and lush, the things it's hard to find in the shops. Be realistic though - there's no way you'll be growing sweet potatoes on your balcony or a mango in a pot, but you could grow a very nice crop of new potatoes and there are few trees prettier in a pot than a peach.

COME UP WITH A GAME PLAN

The great thing about plants, particularly vegetables, is that they really want to grow and will do their best to do so in whatever conditions they're given - just think of the sprouting potatoes and onions you may find in your veg rack! Give plants a helping hand, a nice rich growing spot, some tender loving care and regular watering and they will reward you.

Just because your available space is small doesn't mean it lacks potential - it's up to you to get creative and explore the possibilities. Keep it simple and straightforward to start with and remember you don't want to fill every available space with planting or there won't be any room to move. Take a look at other people's ideas on blogs, Pinterest and other sites for inspiration. If you're in a flat or apartment and only have a windowsill, balcony or patio, then creativity is crucial - and fun, too.

PRACTICALITIES

There are a few things you need to think about before you get going. Sun, wind, watering and soil are all-important to plants.

Watch how the sun moves around your allotted spot - most vegetables need good sunshine to grow well, especially fruiting varieties like tomatoes. Having said that, don't forget that the sun is higher in the sky for longer during the summer months, so if you're mapping out your space during the winter, then remember that the conditions will be brighter for the growing season to come.

Wind can be a real problem, particularly on exposed balconies and in between buildings where it can funnel and whip plants about. Tall plants are especially vulnerable naturally, so choose dwarf varieties of runner/string and French/green beans as well as bush types of tomato rather than the tall cordon types. You can provide wind protection in the form of a purpose-bought windbreak, but clustering pots of plants together is also a good idea as they help to shelter and support one another.

Growing good crops requires regular watering, and plenty of it, throughout the growing season. That's fairly easy when the plants are small with tiny root systems, but the bigger they get, the thirstier they become, especially when they're flowering and setting fruit. Of course you want your plants to be big and fruitful, so think about how you're going to keep up with that constant need for water. Do you need a water butt? Can you set up a hose from your tap/faucet or use your bathwater? How about an automated drip system?

As your plants grow bigger, they'll need potting on into bigger pots and the need for soil or potting compost will also grow. If you live on the fourth floor, bear in mind that's a long way to carry a bag of compost! Big, heavy potted plants might not be a good thing for your balcony or windowsill either as they might be too heavy for the structure, so you might need to tailor your growing plans accordingly.

WHAT TO GROW YOUR PLANTS IN

CONTAINERS

The easiest way to start growing crops in odd spots is in containers, but that doesn't mean they need to be classic garden pots or grow bags. All sorts of items will work as planting containers providing they're large enough to accommodate enough soil for the plant, have good drainage and are clean and non-toxic. After that, you can let your imagination take the lead.

Household items such as large food cans with a few holes drilled into the base work well – in fact, a few tools and offcuts of wood will come in handy. If you have a friendly local restaurant, those giant catering-size olive oil cans are great for tomatoes, flowers and herbs. Also, old baskets, crates and wooden boxes are perfect for salads and leaves, while pallets also make good planters, especially if they're tipped on their side. If you have a bit more space, an old wheelbarrow makes a great container for bigger crops like courgettes/zucchini, which could easily swamp other plants. The great thing about a wheelbarrow container is that you can easily move it about to tidy up or catch the sun.

RAISED BEDS

If you have the space, a raised bed gives you lots of options. You'd be surprised just how much you can fit into a small bed, especially if you plant a new crop as soon as you make space by harvesting another. One bonus of a raised bed is that it allows you to plant crops at greater density and frequency than you would in a normal bed.

Square-foot gardening is an easy-to-manage style of raised bed growing that's both attractive and productive. This is where you mark the bed out into a grid (with each section of the grid measuring a square foot, or 30cm²), planting a different crop or flower in each section.

Raised bed kits are readily available to buy, but making your own is easier than you might think. Use treated timber, old scaffold boards or scrap wood and aim for a minimum depth of 20cm (8in). If you're building on a hard surface rather than having bare earth below, you'll need at least 40cm (16in) to allow for drainage. Make sure the finished bed is small enough that the whole bed is within easy reach for sowing and harvesting.

VERTICAL PLANTING
Successful small space gardening means thinking creatively and making the most of any wall or fence space you have available. Planting vertically allows you to take advantage of the extra space and to make the absolute most of any sunny spots. You can use a pallet planter on the wall or add shelving or brackets for individual pots and containers. Hanging planting pockets are great for salads and herbs, but an old shoe organizer will do just the same job, and you can use a canvas 'bag for life' to hold larger plant pots of tumbling tomatoes.

TOOLS AND KIT
To get started, you'll only need a few tools, such as a trowel, garden fork and perhaps some snips for pruning. You'll also need garden twine for tying in plants and some supports and stakes for taller plants. Canes are the usual choice, but batons of scrap wood will do for training tomatoes or making a wigwam for climbing beans. Use your imagination - I've seen a brilliant show of runner/string beans trained against a fence with a section of concrete reinforcing rebar used as a trellis.

You might want to invest in a small propagator, either heated or unheated, to help your seedlings germinate early in the season. This simply provides a more stable temperature, allowing plenty of light to stimulate the seedlings to germinate but also retaining a moist environment. You can also use cling film, a sealed plastic bag or a sheet of glass to do the same job but it's a bit more fiddly.

Plastic water bottles, especially the big ones, make brilliant cloches for protecting newly planted plants outside, while indoors a clear plastic storage crate makes an excellent greenhouse for getting seedlings started. Instead of plastic pots and seed trays, try collecting old paper cups, toilet roll tubes and egg cartons - they're perfect for starting off plants from seed. Egg cartons are brilliant for setting potatoes to chit (see page 63).

Labelling your crops is useful so you can remember exactly where you have sown seeds and to identify particular varieties later on, especially if they turn out to be good ones you'd like to grow again. The simplest thing to do is to pop the seed packet on a stick and cover it with a clear glass jar to protect it from the rain. But you can also get creative with your labels by using interesting objects as markers - broken plant pots, slate tiles, pebbles and bricks can all be painted, chalked or written on with a permanent laundry marker to make labels. It's a simple and fun way to personalize your odd-spot garden.

GET GROWING

Growing plants from seed is easy and rewarding, but don't start them all off in one go as you'll quickly run out of space. Look at seed packets to see how quickly shoots should appear, so that you can stagger sowing seeds over several weeks.

Some crops you can sow directly outdoors, but many of the tender crops will need starting off inside and possibly pricking out (see page 159) and potting on (see page 158) before you can get them settled outside. That's potentially a lot of windowsill space. You can maximize your window space by adding a couple of temporary shelves in the window, just while everything gets going, of course.

HOW TO SOW OUTDOORS

Sowing outdoors is easy - plants do it naturally, scattering their seed on the ground where they will grow as long as the soil is warm and moist. Generally mid spring to early summer and again in late summer provide the ideal conditions for this, although you can get started earlier with some protection from cloches (see page 158) or adding a layer of horticultural fleece.

You want a good seed sowing surface - this means the soil should be crumbly and moist with no weeds, allowing the seeds to germinate and grow quickly. So prepare the soil by digging it over, breaking up any solid lumps and removing all weeds.

Use a cane or corner of a rake or fork to mark out a shallow groove or 'drill' in the surface - if it's in a pot, the drills will be short. Water the row

before sowing, then thinly scatter seed into the bottom of the drill. Be stingy or you'll be thinning out a lot of wasted plants, as they'll grow too closely together to thrive. Gently tease the soil back over the seeds and label them (see page 14).

HOW TO SOW INDOORS
Sowing indoors gives you the chance to get some tender crops like tomatoes and runner/string beans off to a super early start and gives others that are slow to grow, like celeriac/celery root, a longer season. By the time the weather warms up, they'll be young plants which are big enough to plant outdoors.

Large seeds, like pumpkins and courgettes/zucchini, are easy to deal with as they can be planted individually into pots. Smaller seeds can be planted in shallow seed trays, scattering them thinly over the surface and just covering them lightly with a fine layer of potting compost. These are then pricked out (see page 159) or transplanted into larger pots once they've germinated and they are just big enough to handle. This is called potting on. Use a pencil or a plant label to scoop out a small clump of seedlings with their roots intact, separating them gently and handling them by their leaves. Pot them into cells or individual pots, either singly or as a small clump of seedlings that you can thin out once they're bigger.

PLANTING OUT
Once your indoor grown plants have reached a good size, they will need to be acclimatized to the great outdoors gradually before you can plant them out in their final spots. Don't think about planting outdoors until the risk of frost has passed, which usually means late spring.

Think about just how sheltered and cosseted these plants are indoors; by comparison, outside is harsh, windy, chilly and changeable. The sudden shock could kill off your plants in no time at all. Instead, give them a week or two to toughen up or 'harden off' (see page 159). For the first week move the plants outside into a sheltered spot during the day, covering them with a layer of horticultural fleece to keep them safe from sun scorch and chilly winds, and bring them indoors at night. For the second week remove the fleece and, at the end of the week, leave them out at night with the fleece on as long the weather is kind. After that you can plant them out, perhaps covering them with fleece for a bit longer if the nights are still cold.

A FEW THINGS TO LOOK OUT FOR

Indoor grown seedlings have a nasty but predictable habit of stems becoming a bit long and leggy. You can reduce the likelihood of this by turning the seed trays or pots around regularly as they grow, so the plants don't stretch towards the light in one direction.

Keep your seedlings healthy by fanning them with a newspaper or magazine a couple of times a day. This keeps the air moving around the seedlings and helps to prevent potential 'damping off' or rotting.

Brushing your hand over the seedlings also helps to strengthen the stems, making for tougher, stronger plants in the long run.

Pinch or snip the tips out of some young plants once they're growing strongly. Not all plants benefit from pinching out though, so check the instructions on the seed packet. As a rule of thumb, if you want a plant to focus on getting leafy, strong and bushy as it gets going, then pinch out the uppermost tip to stimulate branching. I do this to climbing and dwarf beans, peas and herbs. It's a good idea for flowers, too.

If you've opted to grow cordon tomatoes (check the packet for the description), you'll need to remove the side shoots as they grow. These varieties need to be trained straight up a cane with no energy going into bushiness whatsoever. Bush tomatoes can be left to grow just as they want - much easier.

PESTS AND DISEASES

Dealing with pests and diseases isn't as fraught as you might think. Plants want to grow and, if they are happy and healthy and growing in the right conditions, they'll be strong and sturdy enough to withstand pests and diseases most of the time. However, if the plants are weak and sickly, then pests and diseases will home in on them. Good conditions, regular watering and feeding all help to prevent these problems getting a grip.

Bear in mind, too, that there are particular times in their lives that plants are vulnerable to attack. When they're young is usually the most likely time, particularly if you've grown them indoors and then planted them out, as they often suffer something of a setback and this makes them more susceptible (see page 19). But don't worry - there are some simple methods of control that are easy to adopt and will safeguard your little darlings.

GROW EXTRA PLANTS
Losing a plant isn't a problem if you have back-up plants to replace them. Always sow a few extra in the ground or in pots, then it's a quick and easy job to replace any sad specimens without leaving gaps.

PLANT RESISTANT VARIETIES
Make the most of the efforts that seed companies and plant breeders have made to help by planting specially bred crops to minimize problems. Blight-resistant potato varieties and carrot-fly resistant carrots increase your chances of beating problems.

PEAK PLANT VULNERABILITY

Plants are really only vulnerable to pests and diseases at particular times in their growing cycles. The main time is when they're young and tender, soft and succulent for aphids and within easy reach of slugs and snails. Get them through this youthful stage and they're well on their way.

Another crucial time is when they're flowering and setting fruit. Any sign of stress due to overheating or lack of water and they become a magnet for pests and diseases, so keep a close eye on them and make sure your watering is thorough and regular.

USE BARRIERS

Creating barriers around your plants to safeguard them is the obvious way to protect them from being eaten by slugs and snails. There are all sorts of materials and methods for making barriers - some of my favourites include using crushed eggshells, sawdust and coffee grounds. A generously heaped circle of these will create a gritty barrier around individual plants that slugs and snails will not want to cross. These need regular topping up, especially if it rains, but once the plants are growing strongly, they can withstand the attention of slugs and snails.

KNOW YOUR ENEMY

Understanding the biology of the common pests and diseases can be really helpful. Many pest populations rise and fall throughout the season, often falling as natural predator populations rise due to the abundance of prey. So be patient, keep a close eye and do all you can to encourage natural predators such as lacewings and ladybirds/ladybugs.

There are some conditions that especially favour certain pests and diseases. For example, blight is more prevalent during mid to late summer in warm, damp weather, so look out for it then or grow early crops to avoid it. Blight is easy to spot as dark brown blotches on the leaves or stems but you need to harvest swiftly once it appears or it will spoil the crop. Also, it's easier for slippery slugs and snails to move around on a rain-slicked patio than a dry, dusty one, so you need to watch out for them in wet weather.

TAKE ACTION
The good thing about slugs and snails is they're large and easy to remove by hand – but be warned they can travel a long way back to your lettuce patch. But slugs also love sweet, yeasty things so that's why beer traps really do work. You can buy a purpose-made beer trap or make your own. Use an old yoghurt or margarine tub, add a little beer and make some holes in the top before burying the beer trap in the ground. Make sure it has a raised lip of at least 2.5cm (1in) so that beetles don't fall into it. Aphids like greenfly and blackfly tend to target weakened, stressed plants and soft growth, but are easily blasted off with a jet of water from a hose.

BE TIDY
Good hygiene is vital; not only does it reduce disease, nipping fungal problems in the bud before they can get a grip, but it also reduces the places that pests can hide. Space your plants so there is air flow around them and they aren't competing for water and light. Also, keep your plants well managed, picking off dead and dying leaves frequently.

CHEMICALS AND HOME-MADE BREWS
Plenty of chemicals exist on the market for dealing with pests and diseases but most of us are veering away from these in favour of organic principles. There are some that are approved for organic use but they should be used sparingly as they kill, rather than deter, pests and may enter the food chain.

Some gardeners have tried making their own concoctions in an effort to reduce using chemicals, but please don't be tempted. These home-brewed mixtures, based on seemingly innocuous dishwashing liquid, essential oils and so on, can actually be harmful to the environment and potentially damage the very plants and creatures they're aiming to protect.

WINDOW GROWING

The first place most people start growing things is on their windowsill. Whether it's a handful of houseplants, a punnet of cress or a tomato plant, the windowsill is a perfect little growing environment. Make the most of this smallest of spaces, both indoors and out. The greenhouse effect of a sunny window is ideal for heat-seeking crops such as bell peppers, chillies and tomatoes, while outside is great for compact-growing culinary herbs and swift salads. What's more handy than a few fresh salad leaves or herbs all within reach of the kitchen?

SMALL BEGINNINGS

Start off small indoors by simply growing some zingy cress on kitchen paper (see page 30) - brilliant for salads and sandwiches. A handful of lush leafy herbs such as basil, chives and parsley are easy to grow and accommodate on even the tiniest windowsill.

GREENHOUSE EFFECT

Choose a windowsill that gets plenty of sun and it will be the perfect indoor growing environment for tender Mediterranean crops like basil, tomatoes, chillies and bell peppers, perhaps even an aubergine/eggplant. The wider the sill, the better as it will be able to accommodate bigger pots and containers (big pots are essential for big leafy growers like aubergines/eggplants and bell peppers). Indoor crops can suffer from getting too steamy and humid so provide ventilation by opening the window on warm days. They can also become a bit lopsided, growing and stretching towards the light, but turning the pots around regularly will help to even up the growth.

THE OUTDOOR WINDOWSILL

Once you incorporate the outside into the equation, your windowsill garden will come on in leaps and bounds. Baby beetroot/beets, salad leaves, edible flowers: the list of what you can grow is considerable and the only restriction is the space available. Don't be too ambitious as overcrowding will only lead to poor yield - the principle with windowsill gardening is to grow just a few things each season so they will have the room and attention to grow well. For example, the best size of pot for growing basil is one with a diameter of at least 15cm (6in), whereas for a couple of dwarf bean plants or some carrots, a container 30cm (12in) deep and wide will suit.

BE SAFE

The bigger and deeper your containers, the better for growing plants but they'll be heavy and prone to getting caught by the wind once they have lots of lush, leafy plants in them. Make sure you've supported them soundly and secured them from falling, especially if using windowsills on upper storeys - don't underestimate just how heavy they will be once they're planted and watered.

ADD COLOUR

Growing a few flowering herbs and edible flowers (see pages 122-23) among your leafy vegetables adds an attractive boost of colour. Those lovely flowers will look great, plus they'll attract those all-important pollinators to your windowsill to fertilize your vegetables.

- spring, summer, autumn, winter
- spring, summer, autumn, winter
- 1-2 weeks
- easy
- full sun or semi-shade
- daily
- 3cm (1¼in)

MICRO-GREENS AND CRESS

The easiest windowsill crop is also one of the tastiest and most versatile. Use cress and micro-greens, which are really sprouted seedlings, to add extra pep to salads and sandwiches. Not only are they quick and easy to grow, but they also have great nutritional value and take up almost no space.

PLANTING

Plain cress (which is actually mustard, strictly speaking) is super easy to grow. Line a tray or container with kitchen paper, wet it thoroughly and sprinkle the seeds over it, lightly pressing them into the paper. (You can grow cress in potting compost if you wish, and it will have a stronger, more mustardy flavour.)

Grow micro-greens such as radish, broccoli, amaranth and kale in pots or trays of potting compost. Pre-soak larger seeds like beetroot/beets for a few hours or overnight, rinsing them before sowing. This speeds up their germination. Cover the seeds lightly with compost and cover with a propagator lid or plastic bag to create a warm, humid environment.

GROWING

Place the container on a drainage tray or saucer on a bright windowsill and water the seeds daily, keeping the paper (or compost) damp at all times. Check the soil by pressing it with your fingers – you're aiming for a moist sponge that should never dry out.

HARVESTING

Cress seedlings should appear within a week, micro-greens may take a little longer and can be snipped with scissors once they're 3–5cm (1½–2in) tall. Cress only needs a couple of seedling leaves to be ready, whereas micro-greens usually have the best flavour once they're showing their first true leaves above the initial seedling leaves.

PESKY PESTS

Once the seedlings germinate, it's best to uncover them so they don't rot. Avoid overwatering for the same reason.

KNOW-HOW

You can grow cress and micro-greens in all sorts of odd containers, such as cleaned egg shells, jam jars, an old colander/strainer, cardboard cartons and quirky crockery for fun projects, or stick to the tried and tested recycled supermarket vegetable trays to make the most of your space.

RECOMMENDATIONS

Cress: mustard cress and curled cress are both easy to grow.

Micro-greens: broccoli, pak choi, beetroot/beets, kale, kohl rabi, chard, radish and peas are all easy, colourful and tasty.

Herb micro-greens: basil, amaranth, chervil, dill and coriander/cilantro are attractive and flavoursome.

CHILLIES

A chilli plant makes a fantastic crop that's both tasty and attractive for a sunny windowsill. One plant can produce dozens of chillies, all with a fantastic flavour and right there when you want to cook with them.

PLANTING

Sow seed in winter or early spring - chillies need a long growing season to perform well. Sow a few seeds into a single pot and place it in a propagator or cover the pot with a plastic bag on a sunny, warm windowsill. Pot the seedlings on into individual pots once they're large enough to handle or, if you only need one or two plants, you can skip this stage and buy ready grown plants - although you won't get the range of varieties you can grow from seed.

GROWING

Grow your chilli plants in pots at least 20cm (8in) deep and wide, either indoors or outside after any risk of frost has passed. Pinch out the growing tip to encourage the plants to branch and bush out. Water regularly, but keep the plants on the dry side to make the chillies hotter. You might need to stake some of the taller varieties, too.

💧	winter, spring
🌱	summer, early autumn
📅	10-16 weeks
🪣	intermediate
☀️	full sun
💦	twice a week
🌱	45cm (18in)
🌰	yes

These sun-lovers really need maximum sunshine and warmth to fruit well so a sunny windowsill is perfect, as is a conservatory, sunny porch, greenhouse or a sunny sheltered spot in the garden. If you're growing indoors, then make sure you open the windows to allow pollinators access to the flowers – or you can impersonate a bee yourself and pollinate by hand, using an artist's paint brush to tickle from flower to flower.

HARVESTING
Chillies are ready to start harvesting from midsummer and the more you pick, the more the plant will produce. Once the weather starts to cool down, you might want to bring any outdoor plants inside to finish off ripening the final crop on a sunny windowsill.

PESKY PESTS
Aphids and whitefly are likely to be the worst problems your chilli plants will encounter and these can be blasted off with a spray of water, paying special attention to the underside of leaves and the growing tips.

KNOW-HOW
Chillies dry and freeze extremely well for long storage. To dry, thread chillies on to a length of twine in an attractive chain and hang in a warm, well-ventilated spot to air dry for a month or so. Alternatively, freeze chillies whole in a plastic bag straight after picking. They will be a little soft when you defrost them but that won't affect the flavour at all.

RECOMMENDATIONS
Apache: hot and juicy chilli that is perfect for pots.

Padrón: the classic tapas variety that is medium hot when green and hotter when it matures to red.

Masquerade: early fruiting with hot chillies in shades of purple, red, yellow and green.

- spring, summer, autumn, winter
- spring, summer, autumn, winter
- 2-3 weeks
- easy
- full sun or semi-shade
- daily
- 7.5cm (3in)

TOP CHOICES

Any peas will do for pea shoots, even the dried peas from the supermarket, as you're not growing them to full-size plants.

PEA SHOOTS

Great for small spaces and super easy for first-time gardeners, pea shoots give you results for little effort.

PLANTING

Soak the dried peas overnight until they swell and lose that hard look. For growing shoots, you can use shop-bought dried peas rather than buying planting seed.

Use a wide container about 6-10cm (2-4in) deep with drainage holes in the bottom - supermarket fruit crates work perfectly. Fill it with compost, scatter the peas on top and cover them lightly with compost, then water.

GROWING

Place in a bright spot - it doesn't need to be especially sunny as peas shoots will also grow happily on a shady windowsill. Check the compost is moist every day and water if needed. The shoots should appear within a week or so and can be for harvested in 2-3 weeks.

HARVESTING

Snip off the shoots above the bottom leaves once they're 7.5cm (3in) or so tall. Some of the shoots should regrow to give you a smaller second harvest.

PESKY PESTS

Avoid overwatering or the seeds will rot - you want the compost to be slightly damp to the touch, but not wet.

KNOW-HOW

You can grow broad/fava beans shoots the same way.

WINDOWSILL TOMATOES

A sunny windowsill makes a great place to grow a pot of tomatoes, provided you choose the right variety and you feed and water well. Vine or cordon tomatoes are grown as a single stem and will need a cane for support, while bush varieties are much easier to manage and look more leafy and attractive.

PLANTING
Plant one or two seeds in individual pots or cells, cover lightly with compost and water. Place them on a bright, sunny windowsill and check the compost daily so it doesn't dry out. The seedlings should germinate quickly – usually within 5-10 days – and will grow swiftly and strongly. They can quickly become leggy and drawn to the light so turn the pots or trays regularly.

GROWING
Pot on into a container that is a minimum of 25cm (10in) deep and wide – ideally your tomato would like the space of a container double that size so, go for the largest container your windowsill can accommodate. When you're potting the plant on, don't be afraid to bury the stem a little deeper than it was beforehand. This will encourage more roots to form and will reduce any 'legginess'.

Place your tomato by the sunniest window you have: a south-facing one is perfect. A deep bay window or a floor-to-ceiling patio door is also ideal as long as it gets

- spring
- summer
- 10 weeks
- intermediate
- full sun or semi-shade
- daily
- 90cm (3ft)
- yes
- yes
- regular feeding

masses of sun each day. Place the pot on a plant saucer or tray as you will be watering every day as well as feeding every week or two with a liquid tomato feed. Don't forget to turn the pots regularly to promote even growth and ripening.

HARVESTING
Harvest tomatoes as they ripen to keep the fruit coming - the more you pick, the more will grow.

PESKY PESTS
Aphids and whitefly are the main pest problems and both are improved by companion planting (see page 59) and good watering and feeding.

KNOW-HOW
Grow your tomato plants alongside some basil, which will not only help to deter aphids but will also prove handy for pasta sauces.

RECOMMENDATIONS
Sungold: supersweet golden tomatoes on a vine or cordon stem.

Gardener's Delight: an old favourite vine or cordon type with brilliant flavour.

Tumbler: bush variety that is brilliant for window boxes and hanging baskets.

Totem: short and stocky bush variety specially bred for containers.

AUBERGINE OR EGGPLANT

Warmth and sun are the key ingredients for growing aubergines/eggplants, which means that cultivating them indoors is possible, although somewhat challenging. There are lots of great small fruiting varieties to grow, as long as you have a suitably sunny window space to devote to a plant.

PLANTING

You'll need to get started early in the year with seed, sowing one or two seeds into a pot and putting them in a heated propagator or a warm place, like the airing cupboard, to germinate as they need at least 21°C (70°F). Young plants are widely available at garden centres and are the easier option if you only have room for one or two plants.

GROWING

It's vital to keep your plants at an even, warm temperature and pot them on when the roots fill the pot they're in. Although you can grow them outdoors in very sheltered, very warm gardens, really the best chance for sunshine and warmth is to grow in a greenhouse or a south-facing window that gets at least 10 hours of sunshine a day.

Pinch out the growing tips at about 45cm (18in) tall and stake as needed. You'll need to pollinate the flowers by hand with an artist's paint brush in the same way

spring

summer

12-16 weeks

challenging

full sun

daily or at least twice a week

90cm (3ft)

yes

regular feeding

as indoor chillies (see page 34) and they will need regular misting with water and regular feeding too. Keeping the plants sufficiently moist is also a challenge, so check every day.

HARVESTING
Pick when the skins are bright and shiny. Check for ripeness by looking under the stem where the fruit joins the plant – it should be white, but if it's green leave it a day or two.

PESKY PESTS
Aubergines/eggplants don't like getting cool, but they also dislike overheating. Temperature is the key factor for success. Plus you need to keep them moist and humid or the flowers can drop off and you won't get a crop. Flea beetles can be a nuisance but raising the plants up above ground level helps to reduce this. Aphids are also a frequent problem but they can be washed off.

KNOW-HOW
Set up a drip watering system or use self-watering pots for best results.

RECOMMENDATIONS
Money Maker No 2: can be grown indoors or out as it will cope with lower temperatures.

Patio Baby: compact, dwarf variety with purple fruit.

Pinstripe: dwarf variety with cream and mauve striped fruit.

HERBS AND SALADS

You don't need a lot of space or sunshine to grow a few leafy lovelies on your windowsill, and these are just what you need to add a little something extra to your meals.

PLANTING
Plant a few seeds of herbs into individual pots or cells, cover lightly with compost and water. The same applies for salads but use a larger container like a small crate or windowbox and sow the seed thinly over the surface.

GROWING
Place them on a bright, sunny windowsill and check the compost daily so it doesn't dry out. Once the seedlings start to grow, turn the pots, boxes or trays regularly so they don't become lopsided. You can also lightly brush them with your hands to strengthen the stems.

HARVESTING
Harvest regularly by snipping some but not all of the plants and snip about 3cm (1¼in) or so above the base to leave some growing points to re-shoot.

PESKY PESTS
Avoid overwatering – check the compost beforehand. Open up the windows for ventilation on warm days too.

KNOW-HOW
Many salads and herbs will grow happily on shadier windowsills as long as it's bright for 3 or 4 hours a day.

💧 spring, summer

🌿 late spring, summer, early autumn

📅 4 weeks

🪴 easy

☀️ semi-shade

💧 weekly

🌱 20cm (8in)

TOP CHOICES
Parsley, mint, chervil, chives and basil are all easy to grow and versatile herbs that are fantastic in the kitchen. Salads such as rocket/arugula, mizuna, mustard and mixed cut-and-come-again leaves are quick and easy to sow time after time.

SMALL GARDENS

Small gardens can be incredibly productive, in part precisely because they're small. A small, compact space is simpler to keep an eye on and manage in terms of watering, weeding and harvesting. It's also easier to spot any problems starting to happen, such as pests, sickly plants or those that aren't getting enough water or light. If you're a busy person, then a small garden is just the right size to look after.

THE IDEAL GARDEN

The key to success is making the most of your available space. There are several ways to do that, but one of the most important things to get right is your layout. Think about your garden: ideally it should be sheltered, sunny for at least half of the day and with rich, deep, fertile soil. You can grow crops directly in the ground or in pots or raised beds, which might take a bit of effort to set up but will pay off in the long run.

RAISED BEDS

These offer the perfect growing space for smaller gardens as you can pack the crops in tightly without losing space to paths. With a good raised bed you can expect to put crops in at just two-thirds of the normal recommended spacing, which means a lot more plants per square metre/yard.

Raised beds will also save you time - a lot of time. Okay, there is an outlay of time and energy at the beginning in getting everything set up, but after that you'll save time on weeding and watering. The plants are packed in closer together than in a conventional garden layout so the weeds will struggle to compete, and it's more efficient to water as there is a small, well-defined area to cover.

POTS AND POTAGERS

As well as raised beds, don't forget that you can grow in pots too. These are perfect for many crops such as small fruit trees because you can move them around to grab the sun in the summer and the best shelter in the winter. See pages 92-120 for more inspiration.

Or make a potager - a decorative vegetable garden of raised beds, trained fruit and edible flowers. This makes a pleasing balance of attractive ornamental garden and productive kitchen garden, which is perfect for many small gardens.

WHAT TO GROW

Fast-growing crops give you quick returns on your efforts. Salad leaves, herbs, kohl rabi and radishes are super fast as well as easy to grow. This will give you a quick turnaround of produce and means you can plant another crop as soon as you harvest.

High-value crops that are difficult to find or can be expensive also make a lot of sense to fit in. It's worth trying out a few plants such as interesting bean varieties, baby vegetables and unusual crops (see pages 144-56).

CLEVER PLANTING

One of the pitfalls of packing plants in more closely is that pests and diseases can become a problem. Choose disease-resistant varieties where possible and companion planting (see pages 59-61) may also help. Don't be tempted to overcrowd your plants - too close and they won't develop properly or they'll bolt and go to seed. You can take a few liberties but don't push your luck too far.

Avoid planting in straight rows and instead opt for squares or even triangles - planting in a triangular pattern means you can fit around ten per cent more plants into a bed, still at the correct spacing.

THINK TALL

Even the smallest garden has a lot of growing potential if you go up. Space-demanding crops can also be some of the tallest and the most fruitful to grow. Think of tomatoes, beans, squashes, cucumber - these can all go up, trained on trellises, canes and stakes. The great thing about vertical planting is that it's also easy to see when things are ready to harvest.

INTER-PLANTING

Planting mutually compatible crops together is an age-old space-saving technique. The 'three sisters' is where sweetcorn, beans and squash are planted together in the same bed: the beans climb up the corn stalks while the squash romps around at ground level, shading out any weeds. Other good combinations include tomatoes with basil and onions, lettuces planted between peas, beans or brassicas, and carrots grown with onions and radishes.

○ spring, summer

❀ late spring, summer, autumn

🗓 10 weeks

🪣 intermediate

☀ full sun

💧 weekly

🌱 10cm (4in)

TOP CHOICES

Flyaway: good resistance to carrot root fly.

Parmex: small round carrots, good for heavier soils.

Nantes: sweet, pointed roots.

CARROTS

Home-grown carrots are the tastiest you'll ever eat. They need deep, light soil to make good roots. Round carrots the size of a ping-pong ball are easier to grow if your soil is heavier due to clay – they're cute, too.

PLANTING

Sow seeds in spring once the weather warms up. Sow the small seeds about 5cm (2in) apart in shallow rows which are about 20cm (8in) apart. Cover lightly with soil, watering them in to settle the soil. The seeds should germinate within a couple of weeks.

GROWING

Avoid thinning the seedlings to prevent carrot root fly, but if necessary thin to 5cm (2in) apart. Water only if very dry, as water on foliage will attract carrot root fly.

HARVESTING

Pull your carrots after rain or watering, as they'll slip out of the ground easily without breaking off.

PESKY PESTS

Slugs and snails can be a problem at the seedling stage, but it's carrot root fly that will ruin your crop. Choose a resistant variety, sow early in the season or cover them with fleece or mesh to deter the pesky fly.

KNOW-HOW

Companion planting (see pages 59-61) really helps to ward off carrot root fly. Try inter-planting with garlic, radishes and onions to mask the smell of the carrots.

CHARD

The most plentiful crop of greens you can grow, chard keeps on cropping all summer long. It's easier to grow than spinach, low maintenance and looks great. Grow it in a potager (see page 49), raised beds or pots.

PLANTING
Sow seeds thinly about 1.5cm (½in) deep and in rows about 30cm (12in) apart. Once the seedlings appear, thin to 20cm (8in) apart to allow the plants to develop fully. Use the thinnings for salads.

GROWING
All chard should need is some water during dry spells.

HARVESTING
Treat this as a cut-and-come-again crop, harvesting the outer, older leaves and leaving the centre of the plant to keep growing. Use younger leaves in salads, older ones for stir-fries or as a green vegetable.

PESKY PESTS
Slugs and snails can be a problem at the seedling stage, so try adding grit around the plants (see page 24). Chard can be prone to bolting so make sure your spacing is adequate and keep the plants hydrated.

KNOW-HOW
Established chard plants will frequently overwinter to give you a quick spring crop before running to seed.

 spring, summer

late spring, summer, autumn

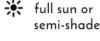 10-12 weeks

easy

 full sun or semi-shade

weekly

45cm (18in)

TOP CHOICES
Bright Lights: my favourite with stems of orange, pink, white and red with lush green leaves.

Bright Yellow: reliable with sunny yellow stalks.

- spring, early summer
- summer, autumn
- 10 weeks
- intermediate
- full sun or semi-shade
- weekly
- 1.8m (6ft)
- yes
- yes

CLIMBING OR POLE BEANS

Beans are one of the most fruitful – and prettiest – crops you can grow in a small area. In a small garden you can afford space for climbing varieties that will keep your kitchen well stocked in beans for the whole season, not to mention freezing some for winter too. Besides the usual runner/string beans and French/green beans, there are speckled borlotti/cranberry beans to try, too.

PLANTING
Sow seeds indoors or outside. I find the best success is sowing single seeds 5cm (2in) deep in individual pots indoors in spring and planting them out once the risk of frost has passed in late spring. Alternatively, sow outdoors in late spring. Either way, the seeds should germinate within a couple of weeks.

GROWING
Pinch out the tips once they're 10cm (4in) tall to encourage branching. Harden off (see page 19) before planting out if you've grown them indoors. Once they get going, beans are easy to grow although support is crucial. Use a wigwam or a trellis around 1.5-2m (5-6½ft) tall and space the plants 15cm (6in) apart.

HARVESTING
Pick beans regularly every few days to keep them producing new beans. Once the seeds within the beans begin to swell, they tend to stop flowering and fruiting.

PESKY PESTS

Slugs and snails are real problem at the young plant stage and it's worth having a few back-up plants at a ready in case you lose some. Slug traps and grit circles (see pages 24-25) around each plant work well, and once they're off and climbing they'll be fine.

KNOW-HOW

Inter-plant with a quick crop of lettuces or salad leaves that will appreciate the shade from these tall bean varieties.

RECOMMENDATIONS

Borlotti/cranberry bean 'Lingua di Fuoco': suited to colder climates with beautiful red speckled pods and beans.

Runner/string bean 'Painted Lady': highly ornamental Victorian variety with red and white flowers followed by tender beans.

French/green bean 'Cosse Violette': my favourite variety with deep purple straight pods and mauve flowers.

COMPANION PLANTING

Gardening in odd spots inevitably means packing plants in close together to make the most of every bit of space. With some clever thinking you can put those plants together to the benefit of all. Companion planting works on several levels: maximizing the space available, reducing the effects and incidence of pests, bringing in the pollinators, and looking good, too.

BRILLIANT BLOOMS
Flowers aren't just for looking pretty. Nasturtiums are great for luring aphids and cabbage white butterflies away from your bean and cabbage crops, while calendula are brilliant for attracting pollinators to your courgette/zucchini and pumpkin flowers. Flowering herbs such as chives and thyme attract pollinators, while their strongly scented foliage also repels aphids and blackfly.

USE YOUR BEANS
Position tall growing French/green and runner/string beans where they can help to shade other plants that are prone to bolting, such as lettuces and spinach, while dwarf beans make a great weed suppressant in between rows of potatoes.

MIX IT UP

Avoid planting a lot of one thing en masse. That's easy if you're planting in pots and containers, but in a bed try to go for short rows and a few flowers. Mixing it up makes it harder for pests to locate their favourite plants in the first place, giving them less chance to get established and spread throughout your crop.

Also, dot odd crops in between slower growers such as brassicas. A speedy crop of radishes or lettuce makes the most of your limited space and keeps the weeds at bay.

PLANT VEG TOGETHER

Sowing a few spring onions/scallions along with your carrots will help to deter carrot fly - and the carrots put off onion fly, too. The same applies to leeks. Tomatoes look great planted with a few French marigolds, but the marigolds' pungent foliage also repels any whitefly. Chives are also helpful in deterring aphids from tomatoes - and your roses, too.

BRING IN THE BIRDS

Planting bird- and wildlife-friendly plants does more than simply attract the birds so you can see them. Once they're in your garden, the birds will have a good tidy up of any pests lurking about. Lacewings, ladybirds/ladybugs and other predatory insects will also be drawn to the aphids and other pests in the garden.

POTATOES

There's something about growing your own potatoes that makes you feel you're a true gardener. A handful of potato plants won't take up much space but will give you a surprisingly fruitful crop and an even greater sense of pride.

PLANTING

Potatoes are grouped in three categories in order of harvest: first early, second early and main crop. Main crop potatoes are harvested in high summer and planted in mid to late spring, whereas the early varieties are planted early in spring and so need starting off or 'chitting' indoors to get them underway. These can be harvested from early summer for early season 'new' potatoes or even late spring for baby potatoes.

Chitting just means getting the potatoes to sprout and it can be started in late winter about 6 weeks before you want to plant your potatoes out in the ground. Set the blunt, more rounded end of the potatoes upright in an old egg carton on a bright windowsill and, once the sprouts are 1.5-2.5cm (½-1in) long, they're ready to plant.

Dig a trench 10cm (4in) or so deep and carefully place the potatoes, with the chitted (or sprouting) end upwards, 30cm (12in) apart, gently covering them with soil. Allow a bit more space between potatoes for the later harvesting varieties as they grow for longer and get bigger, and about 40cm (16in) between the rows.

spring, summer

spring, summer, autumn

3-4 weeks

easy

full sun

weekly

90cm (3ft)

GROWING

As the shoots appear, gently mound up the soil to cover them. Keep doing this 'ridging up' through the season until the potatoes have a mound about 15cm (6in) or so above them.

HARVESTING

Early 'new' potatoes should be ready for lifting as the summer begins, the others can be left for longer. You can tell they're ready once the flowers open. The second earlies and main crop varieties can be left until later in the summer, but keep an eye open for potato blight.

PESKY PESTS

Potato blight, a fungal disease, is the main problem but you can avoid this by sticking to early and second early varieties that are harvested before blight usually becomes an issue in late summer. You can spot blight easily by the distinctive brown splodges on the stems and leaves - get them out of the ground quickly before it affects the crop.

Make sure you water if it's dry, especially once the potatoes are growing strongly, or the crop could be small. Potato scab can also affect potato plants that struggle for water, although it doesn't harm the potatoes for eating. You can't see the scab affecting the plant as such, although it's easy to spot if your potato plants need watering, so keep them hydrated.

KNOW-HOW

Don't try to grow supermarket potatoes, even if they are sprouting in your vegetable basket. They're often treated with growth inhibitors to stop them sprouting, whereas 'seed' potatoes from the nursery or garden centre are certified free of disease and are ready to grow.

RECOMMENDATIONS

Cherie: my favourite first early with pink skin and firm yellow flesh.

Chieftain: early, with good disease resistance.

Nicola: second early with good disease resistance, producing attractive oval potatoes.

Vivaldi: great second early variety that can be left longer and treated as a main crop.

Sarpo Mira: a blight resistant late maincrop variety that stores well into autumn and winter.

Apache: a colourful and tasty early maincrop variety that has become one of my favourites.

SUMMER SALADS

Salad leaves are one of those ingredients that are brilliant harvested fresh from the garden. Lovely lettuces, tangy mizuna and mustards are soft and succulent when freshly picked, but quickly go limp and lacklustre if shop-bought and stored in the fridge. Grow individual varieties or a salad leaf mix in pots, crates, raised beds - anything that comes to hand.

PLANTING

Sow indoors to get them off to a good start in spring, planting out later after the frost risk has passed. Later in summer you can sow directly into the ground, with the last sowing in late summer. Sow every 3 weeks or so to ensure a consistent supply.

GROWING

Salads need generous watering through the season, ideally in the evening to prevent the leaves scorching and to conserve moisture.

HARVESTING

Snip the leaves when they're 10-15cm (4-6in) tall, cutting at least 2.5cm (1in) above the surface to allow them to regrow (a growing technique known as 'cut-and-come-again'). Water the plants afterwards and they should be big enough to harvest again after a couple of weeks. You should be able to do this three or four times before the plants become exhausted.

spring, summer

spring, summer, autumn

3-4 weeks

easy

semi-shade

twice a week

15cm (6in)

PESKY PESTS

Salads draw slugs and snails like a magnet, so get your beer trap (see page 25) ready before you sow. Grit or eggshells around plants (see page 24) or in between rows will also help. Remove dead and dying leaves swiftly too, to stop any fungal diseases and rots spreading.

KNOW-HOW

All sorts of herbs, flowers and leaves can be added to your summer salads such as nasturtiums, chives, chervil, land cress, beetroot/beet and even some weeds such as dandelion and garlic mustard.

RECOMMENDATIONS

Mizuna: spiky, peppery, soft leaves.

Mustard 'Red Giant': large, red leaves that are so powerful you'll only need a few

Lettuce 'Green Salad Bowl': a brilliant cut-and-come-again classic lettuce variety.

Salad rocket/arugula: milder and softer than wild rocket/arugula.

BEETROOT OR BEET

Beetroot/beet is one of the simplest crops to grow in pots or raised beds. Eat some of the young leaves as an early salad crop, followed by the bulbous roots later on.

PLANTING
Sow the knobbly seeds 7.5cm (3in) apart from one another and 3cm (1¼in) deep. Several plants will sprout as they're actually clusters of seeds, so thin to one seedling once they're 2.5cm (1in) or so tall. Use the thinnings as salad leaves.

GROWING
Beetroot/beet like a fertile soil and regular watering. Add organic matter such as compost to the soil before planting and water every 10 days in dry weather.

HARVESTING
Start harvesting the roots when they're the size of a ping-pong ball, choosing every other root to allow the others to grow on a little.

PESKY PESTS
Beetroot are prone to bolting, so choose one of the bolt-resistant varieties to be on the safe side.

KNOW-HOW
The traditional colour for beetroot is the classic 'beetroot red', but there's a rainbow of beets available from deep purple-blue to yellow, cream and even white.

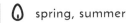 spring, summer

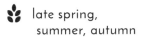 late spring, summer, autumn

 7 weeks

 easy

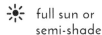 full sun or semi-shade

 weekly

 15cm (6in)

TOP CHOICES
Chioggia: beautiful striped white and pink roots.

Boltardy: a bolt-resistant variety.

Bull's Blood: deep red leaves that are great for salads, followed by baby beets.

SPACE SAVERS

Small spaces call for clever and well-planned planting and some crops are better to grow than others when space is tight. It's worth making a sowing calendar to keep you on track - a simple week-by-week list will remind you of what needs to be done. My favourite method is to date blank envelopes with the optimum planting months and pop the seed packets inside so I work my way through, month by month.

FREQUENT CROPPERS
Space savers include those speedy-to-grow crops that can be sown time after time in succession to keep those crops coming. Ideally you need to sow a few seeds every couple of weeks for regular supplies of all those baby vegetables such as beetroots/beets, turnips and carrots.

Space savers also include many of the cut-and-come-again favourites such as salad leaves and stir-fry mixes. These usually involve at least two sowings per season - one in spring and a second in summer - as the regular cropping tends to exhaust the plants. Eventually they do what all stressed plants do - they go to seed and fade away - by which time your next sowing is ready to crop.

MINIATURE VARIETIES
Seed companies have also recognized the fact that those of us with tiny gardens and smaller households still want to grow vegetables and they are now developing super dwarf compact varieties that offer brilliant value for the smallest of spaces. Old favourites such as cabbages and lettuces were bred to be bigger and leafier back in the days when there were a lot of mouths to feed. Nowadays it's mini varieties the size of an orange that we wish to grow, perfect miniatures that we can pack tightly into a small garden and that will be just right for one or two meals.

ROOM FOR FRUIT

Growing fruit in a small space is also very achievable, especially if you use your walls and fences. With a bit of horticultural know-how it's easy to train fruit trees, such as apples and pears, to grow flat against a vertical surface (so they take up minimal space and don't grow outwards into the garden). These often crop well due to the sunlight, warmth and air that can get to the fruit, ripening it beautifully. If you have a south- or west-facing fence or wall that is especially sheltered, you could even consider growing a fan-trained peach or fig (i.e. the branches all fan upwards from the central trunk).

Almost all fruits can be trained on a wall or fence: redcurrants, gooseberries and blackberries all look great and fruit wonderfully. Strawberries will do well in racks or pocket planters on a sturdy fence or wall. Alternatively, you could opt for a specially bred dwarf variety of fruit tree – many of these are also specially selected for growing in patio containers. As well as the usual apples, pears, peaches and so on, there are even 'standard' or mini tree varieties of fruit bushes such as redcurrants that look great in smaller pots and containers.

USE YOUR WALLS

When it comes to those walls and fences, don't just think about fruit, though. Even some of the really big growers such as runner/string and French/green beans will thrive growing up a fence or wall, covering it all summer long with lush leaves, pretty flowers and plenty of edible pods.

- ◐ spring, summer
- ❀ late spring, summer, autumn, winter
- ▤ 6-8 weeks
- ▽ intermediate
- ☀ full sun
- ◁ weekly
- ⇈ 15cm (6in)

MINI CABBAGES

Mini varieties of the humble cabbage come in all shapes and forms, including the classic Savoy, ball-head and pointed varieties. Cabbages are versatile vegetables with many varieties cropping all year round.

PLANTING

Cabbage seeds can be sown either directly into a seedbed or started off in growing cells or seed trays under cover. Sow thinly and thin the plants out to 7.5cm (3in) apart as they develop. Germination usually takes 1-2 weeks and the seedlings are ready for transplanting when they have 5-6 leaves.

GROWING

Use a dibber to make a hole in the soil large enough to accommodate the root ball and firm the soil around the plant. Spacing between plants varies - for compact heads space at 30cm (12in), whereas pointed spring varieties need only 15cm (6in) between them to encourage their conical shape.

HARVESTING

Spring cabbage is planted in early spring for mature heads later in the season. The same applies for summer varieties while winter cabbages, including many Savoy varieties, are sown in late spring and early summer for cutting throughout the winter. Red cabbages are ready from late summer and, although they won't overwinter in the ground, they do store well.

PESKY PESTS

Cabbages need protecting from slugs, pigeons and caterpillars, all of which will attempt to devour the crop before you can. Cover the plants with fleece or very fine netting to protect them from birds and butterflies and use slug traps (see page 25). Keep a close eye on the developing plants so you can spot any caterpillar activity and deal with them swiftly by picking them off by hand, or use a nematode biological control.

KNOW-HOW

After harvesting cut a cross 1cm (½in) deep in the stump of spring and summer cabbages and you'll be rewarded with a second crop of much smaller cabbages later in the year.

RECOMMENDATIONS

Minicole F1: a classic ball-head variety.

Katarina F1: another ball-head form.

Alcosa F1: Savoy variety with classic crinkled leaves.

Ruby Ball F1: small red ball cabbage.

STRAWBERRIES

Strawberries are the first treasured fruits of summer and, given the right conditions, they're rewarding and easy to grow. Grow the big, luscious varieties that will give you an early harvest or try a perpetual fruiting variety for small but steady crops throughout the summer.

PLANTING

Strawberries are best planted as young plants or as 'runners' from older plants (these are the long stems that shoot out, with small leaves and roots at the end – leave these attached to the plant, but pin them down in the soil so the roots can become established, at which point you can snip through the trailing stem).

Strawberry plants have shallow root systems and all varieties need copious amounts of watering and regular feeding every couple of weeks throughout their growing and fruiting season.

GROWING

Classic varieties are sun-lovers, but the tiny alpine varieties will grow happily as ground cover in shade.

There are three easy ways to grow strawberries in a small space: as trailing plants in a hanging basket, racks or wall planters; as a climbing plant trained onto a frame, or in those classic pots you see at garden centres, featuring pockets for planting.

spring, early autumn

summer

8 weeks

intermediate

full sun

2 or 3 times a week

15cm (6in)

runners

weekly

For baskets, use the deepest basket you can find and aim for no more than 4 plants, while pocket planters will often accommodate up 8 plants. Climbing strawberries will need tying in to the framework to train them.

Try to avoid wetting the leaves when watering as this can lead to rot. Use a seep hose (see page 104) if possible or water early in the day so the foliage can dry off.

HARVESTING
The best time to pick strawberries is during the warmest part of the day because this is when they are at their most tasty. Pick when they are bright red all over and test a couple of fruits for flavour to make sure they're ripe. Eat them as soon as possible because home-grown varieties don't keep well once they're ripe.

PESKY PESTS
Birds love strawberries so protect the developing fruit with a net. Any fruit hanging close to the ground will be a magnet for slugs, but tucking straw under the plants lifts the fruit away from the soil and makes it difficult for slugs to reach.

KNOW-HOW
Growing a handful of single, open-flowered annuals such as calendula nearby will help to attract bees, which will pollinate your strawberry plants and improve the fruiting.

RECOMMENDATIONS
Mignonette: an alpine variety ideal for hanging baskets with small, sweet berries.

Cambridge Favourite and **Honeoye:** both are classic summer fruiters.

Mara des Bois and **Ostara:** perpetual fruiting forms.

Mount Everest and **Rambling Cascade:** both produce long trailing stems ideal for training on a frame or trailing from a wall rack.

- spring, summer
- late spring, summer
- 6 weeks
- easy
- full sun or semi-shade
- twice a week
- 15cm (6in)
- weekly

MINI LETTUCES

Summer is all about home-grown lettuces freshly harvested for a crisp salad, but many varieties are just too big and end up languishing limply in the fridge. Little Gem/Boston has become hugely popular in the shops precisely because it's not too big, but there are mini varieties you can grow yourself that are just the right size.

PLANTING
Lettuce seed can generally be sown from early spring onwards, with a cloche for protection if needed. Germination normally takes 14–21 days. Alternatively, you can start seeds in pots or trays indoors and plant outdoors in spring.

GROWING
Thinning outdoor sown lettuce seedlings can begin as soon as the first true leaves appear, and do this gradually, continuing until the plants are spaced 30cm (12in) apart. Don't forget the larger seedlings can be picked and eaten. Regular watering is crucial to growing good lettuces. Unless it rains, water well at least once a week and more often during periods of hot weather.

HARVESTING
Repeat sowing throughout the season will keep the harvests coming but don't overestimate how many lettuces you will need, as they don't stand well in the ground and need to be eaten once they're ready.

Ideally, plant lettuce in raised beds or grow bags to maximize production, although you can easily grow a couple of plants at a time in containers, depending on the size of the pot. Raised beds and containers warm up faster than the surrounding ground, so you should be able to get an earlier start in the spring and a later crop in the autumn. The open ground is colder and more of a haven for pests such as slugs and snails.

PESKY PESTS
Slugs are the main problem for young seedlings, so make the most of beer traps (see page 25). You can also use sawdust or broken eggshells (see page 24) to create barriers around plants. You may also need to protect young lettuce from birds with horticultural fleece or fine netting.

KNOW-HOW
Make the most of your space by planting lettuce around taller plants like broccoli, Brussels sprouts and beans. The lettuce helps its neighbours by keeping the surrounding soil moist and cool and shading weeds out. Then, as the taller plants grow, they provide shade for the lettuce during the warmer days of summer.

RECOMMENDATIONS
Little Gem: the classic baby lettuce similar to cos/romaine. Also known as Boston lettuce.

Set: a crisp leaf variety.

Tom Thumb: a small butterhead form that is ideal for small spaces.

RADISHES

Without doubt the radish is the easiest of all vegetable plants to grow and it's also super quick to crop, as well as tolerant of all sorts of soils and conditions.

PLANTING
Sow throughout spring, summer and early autumn at regular intervals in free spots in the garden or in containers. Sow radish seed direct into the ground but only sow a few at a time, as they'll quickly get woody if left too long in the ground.

GROWING
Radishes prefer warm soil so don't sow too early in spring. They need plenty of moisture for healthy growth and regular watering is a must. Thin out seedlings to 5cm (2in) apart if sown close together to encourage individual plants to form roots. You may need to increase this spacing up to 10cm (4in) for larger varieties such as mooli/daikon.

HARVESTING
Summer radishes should be ready to harvest after about 3 weeks. Winter cultivars can be harvested from early winter onwards.

spring, summer, autumn

late spring, summer, autumn, winter

3-6 weeks

easy

full sun or semi-shade

weekly

7.5cm (3in)

PESKY PESTS

Young radishes attract slugs and snails but using a band or circle of grit will help to deter them see page 24). Older plants can be affected by flea beetle - look out for a speckling of holes in the leaves. The best method of prevention is to grow under horticultural fleece. Regular feeding with a water-on fertilizer will also help, as strong plants are more able to fend off pests.

KNOW-HOW

When thinning radishes, you can add the young leaves to salads as a micro-green.

RECOMMENDATIONS

French Breakfast: a classic old variety with pink and white, peppery roots.

Plum Purple: unusual bright purple skin and white flesh with a sweet but spicy flavour.

Ping Pong: round, white roots and a slightly milder flavour.

April Cross: winter variety with long white roots up to 30cm (12in) long. It's a type of Japanese mooli/daikon, which is good in salads or stir-fries.

- spring, summer
- late spring, summer, autumn, winter
- 6-8 weeks
- easy
- full sun
- weekly
- 15cm (6in)

TOP CHOICES

White Lisbon: the classic spring onion; tasty and quick to crop.

Ishikura: long white variety that doesn't form bulbs.

Apache: its rich purple-red stems can add variety to salads.

SPRING ONIONS OR SCALLIONS

These versatile vegetables are easy to grow throughout the season and any you don't use straight away can be left in the ground to 'bulb up' and become larger.

PLANTING
Because they are harvested before they mature, there's no need to dedicate as much space as you would for regular onions. Simply sow seed 15cm (6in) apart in shallow drills from spring to early summer.

GROWING
Spring onions can rot in a waterlogged soil, so make sure to plant them in well-drained ground, and be careful not to over-water. All onions hate competition from weeds so keep the ground clear and tidy.

HARVESTING
Both the green tops and small white bulb are edible and their flavour is much milder than mature onions.

PESKY PESTS
Remarkably untroubled by pests, the only thing you might need to do is to protect the young seedlings from birds with fleece, netting or cloches.

KNOW-HOW
Also known as salad onions, spring onions/scallions are simply immature onions, which are harvested before the bulb has had a chance to swell.

KOHL RABI

This member of the cabbage family looks like a turnip which gives it its unusual name: in German kohl means cabbage and rabi means turnip. It's incredibly versatile and forgiving of poor soil and a dubious location, too.

PLANTING
Sow the green and white varieties from mid spring to midsummer for summer cropping, while the hardier purple varieties can be sown from midsummer for autumn and winter crops. Sow little and often, directly into the ground, every few weeks, for a constant supply.

GROWING
Take care not to plant cell-grown plants too deeply – it's the bulbous stem that will actually become the crop, so don't cover it with soil. Although these are drought resistant, they will still need watering during dry spells.

HARVESTING
Harvest kohl rabi when their swollen stems are small and tender – ideally golf/tennis-ball size – or they'll become tough. You can harvest into winter, just avoid the coldest months, and the leaves are edible, too.

PESKY PESTS
Net or fleece young plants to protect them against birds and cabbage root fly.

KNOW-HOW
Kohl rabi is far more drought resistant, easier and quicker to grow than many brassicas such as swedes (rutabaga).

spring, summer

late spring, summer, autumn, winter

7-8 weeks

easy

full sun or semi-shade

weekly

15cm (6in)

TOP CHOICES
Kongo: quick growing, sweet, juicy and high yielding.

Blusta: fast maturing and resistant to bolting.

Superschmelz: mild, sweet tasting white cultivar, remains tender whatever the size.

Domino: an early variety, good for growing under cover early in the season.

CROPS IN POTS

There is almost no limit to the variety of crops you can grow in pots, given a large enough container, some horticultural know-how and a good helping of tender loving care. However, there are crops that simply grow better and more happily in pots than others, which makes them perfect for the smaller space. Many of these plants such as tomatoes will also appreciate the controlled environment of a pot and the lack of weed competition and greater water retention that a pot can offer.

LOCATION, LOCATION, LOCATION

Most fruits and vegetables are sun-lovers, which means they need a full day of sun to really give their best in terms of cropping. There's no two ways about this, although there are a handful of vegetables and fruits that will contend with lower light levels such as runner/string beans and currants. Equally there are some like tomatoes that will not perform unless they have unadulterated sunshine for a good 6 hours a day. It's easy to think that your garden or balcony gets more sun than it actually does, so keep an eye on the sun levels before and during the growing season, placing your pots and plants accordingly.

TOPS OF THE POTS

Choosing containers is always a tricky business but the general rule is the bigger, the better. The bigger and deeper your container, the more water it will hold. Water is a must-have for container-grown vegetables and the most likely reason they will fail is through lack of water. Also, the more soil and compost the container can hold, then the more available the nutrients and the greater stability your plants will gain.

Pots, troughs and grow bags are all perfect but almost anything can be used, as long as it has adequate drainage and is deep enough. Grow bags aren't deep and so are only good for shallower rooting crops such as salads. In general, aim for an absolute minimum of 45cm (18in) depth or you'll be constantly watering and feeding.

SOIL AND COMPOST

Most shop-bought multi-purpose composts will work for growing all sorts of vegetables. Grow bags, too, are often cheap but of good enough quality for many crops. But for longer-term crops such as fruit trees, a soil-based compost such as John Innes No 3 will prove longer lasting and more robust. Bear in mind the weight of the compost, especially if you have to carry it up several flights of stairs. JI No 3 is decidedly heavier than a multi-purpose type. You can make your own mixture with two parts soil and one part well-rotted organic matter with a dash of slow-release fertilizer, although you will get a few weeds popping up. Shop-bought composts are heat treated to kill off any weed seeds.

WATERING

Watering is the key to success with container growing fruit and vegetables. The crucial thing is to make sure you water regularly and consistently - erratic watering causes as many problems as too little or too much watering. Automatic watering systems offer a brilliant solution and can be expanded or adapted to suit most container gardens. Alternatively, you can buy self-watering planters, which are an expensive but practical solution, especially if you are away frequently. Earthbox and Grow Box both make great self-watering vegetable containers.

In your enthusiasm to retain water in your pots, don't be tempted to block up the drainage holes. A plant sitting in stagnant water will swiftly die, so make sure the pot is well drained and ideally raised on pot feet or a couple of batons of wood to allow excess water to drain freely.

Before watering, check if the soil is moist by pushing your finger into the compost as far as your second knuckle - if it's dry, then water. Gauging how much to water is a tricky business - wind, heat, humidity, compost and the size of the pot all play a part in how swiftly a plant will dry out. But when you do water, water thoroughly, waiting for the water to appear at the base of the pot before moving on to the next plant.

As a rule of thumb, a large tomato plant in the height of the season will need watering once a day - possibly twice - and the same will be true of most things in fruit or flower.

FEEDING

Most composts and potting soils contain few nutrients and those are often swiftly used up in those first weeks after final potting. Feeding adds the essential ingredients that all plants need to grow and fruit successfully and, while plants grown in the ground often need a boost, the nutrients are absolutely vital to the success of pot-grown crops. There are lots of fertilizers to choose from, but a slow-release form that you can mix in with the potting compost is an easy option. Add to that a liquid feed every week or two and your plants will be bursting with vigour.

OVERCROWDING

When you have a veritable forest of seedlings to choose from, it might seem like a good idea to plant a few extra plants in each container but it's usually counterproductive. Unless the container is a decent size, too many plants can cause unhealthy competition which exhausts the plants and can lead to them bolting or going to seed without really producing. There are a few exceptions such as salads where the thinnings can provide a tasty meal in their own right, but overcrowding is generally to be avoided.

STAKING AND WIND

Wind can play havoc with container-grown plants so locate your pots with as much shelter as possible. Walls, fences and other plants can all provide good shelter, as can grouping containers together for mutual protection.

Staking is also crucial to protect those fragile stems from breaking, especially once they're laden with fruit. Tomatoes, tall growing beans and trained fruit will all need robust support throughout their potted lives. Bamboo canes and batons of wood will do the job, but for a more attractive option take a look at ready-made frames and stakes from the garden centre.

USE YOUR WALLS

Don't forget that walls and fences offer great opportunities for pots and containers such as herbs pots on shelving or brackets, flower pockets of salads and trellises of climbing beans.

- 🌢 spring
- ❧ summer, autumn
- 📅 8-10 weeks
- 🪣 intermediate
- ☀ full sun
- 🫗 daily or twice a week
- ↑↑ 1.2m (4ft)
- 🌑 weekly

TOMATOES

Tomatoes are often the first crop you ever grow as a beginner gardener. Rightly so, as there is nothing that beats picking your very own sun-warmed tomato from your very own plant. Not only that, but the flavour of home-grown tomatoes and the sheer range of varieties that you can grow makes tomatoes a must-have crop.

Tomatoes come in two basic types: bush and cordon. Bush are by far the easiest to grow, especially outdoors as they don't need staking and training, whereas cordon varieties need careful thinning and staking or stringing up, which makes them better suited to indoor growing. For the ornamental garden, bush varieties are far more attractive than spindly cordons but the more unusual varieties often tend to be cordon types.

PLANTING
You can buy ready-grown young plants but if you want to grow the more unusual varieties you'll probably need to start from seed. Sow from late winter to early spring, putting a few seeds each 1cm (½in) deep into small pots. Water and place the pots on a warm, bright windowsill or in a propagator and, once they germinate, thin to the strongest seedling in each pot.

GROWING
Grow outdoors in a warm, sheltered spot against a sunny wall or fence and water regularly, aiming for a couple of gallons per plant per week. Feed with a high potash fertilizer weekly to encourage flowering and fruiting.

Bush tomatoes can be left to grow as they would like, only removing a few leaves if necessary to allow sun to get to the fruit to ripen it properly.

Cordon tomatoes need staking to a tall cane and all the side shoots should be removed regularly to concentrate the growth into the main stem. Allow only four trusses of flowers and fruits to develop before pinching out the top of the plant to stop its upward growth.

HARVESTING

Harvest fruits as they ripen – around 7–8 weeks after planting for bush types and a further 2–3 weeks for cordon types.

PESKY PESTS

Besides aphids and whitefly, the worst problems outdoor grown tomatoes face are cultural problems caused by erratic watering, such as blossom end rot, fruit splitting and greenback where hard green patches appear near the stalk and which is also due to overheating. The other major problem towards the height of the summer is blight, the same fungal problem that also affects potatoes, which is more prevalent in wet summers and on stressed plants.

KNOW-HOW

Tomatoes aren't always red – you can get yellow, orange, pink, purple and even black and white tomatoes. In fact, there are around 10,000 different varieties of tomato worldwide, which makes picking favourites difficult.

Tomatoes are lycopene-rich, which is good for the heart and helps to prevent some cancers.

RECOMMENDATIONS

Gardener's Delight: a classic cherry variety with fantastic flavour and a great choice for containers and grow bags.

Sungold: my top choice for flavour and good looks, this golden large cherry is a cordon variety and needs a roomy pot but it's well worth the extra hassle.

Tumbler: a brilliant tumbling variety for containers and hanging baskets.

Losetto: a modern blight-resistant variety with masses of cherry fruits.

FRUIT BUSHES

A surprising variety of fruit bushes grow very successfully in pots, and, with their leafy rounded shape, they look great in quirky containers like old buckets or troughs.

PLANTING

Choose varieties that are specially bred for growing in pots and remember that you'll need a good-sized pot – for most fruits that's 40-50cm (16-20in) in diameter and about the same depth. You can use a smaller container, but you'll need to re-pot after a year or so. Make sure your container has adequate drainage holes – you don't want your plant to get waterlogged – or plant in a plastic pot with predrilled drainage holes and place inside your bucket or other container.

GROWING

Blackcurrants, redcurrants, blueberries and gooseberries are all great to grow in containers and they're rather attractive too. Grow your fruits in a good, sunny spot if possible as you'll get the best crops, but don't forget that you'll need to water and feed your plants regularly. Gooseberries are brilliantly productive in pots – they like a bit of air around them so it's easy to reposition the pot as necessary and they'll also fruit in light shade too. Blueberries need acidic soil to thrive, which is simple to provide in a pot – buy a bag of ericaceous compost at the garden centre. They're a great choice for pots as their leaves turn lovely shades in the autumn, too.

spring, summer

spring, summer, autumn, winter

40-52 weeks

challenging

full sun or semi-shade

weekly

75cm (2½ft)

yes

HARVESTING

Harvesting starts in midsummer but can go on for some time as smaller berries start to ripen. It's a good idea to thin gooseberries in early summer to allow the remaining fruits to get bigger. You can stew the thinned fruits but, be warned, they'll be somewhat sharp.

PESKY PESTS

The main problem you're likely to face is mildew due to the plants drying out. Keep them well watered and fed throughout the season, particularly when flowering and fruiting, and look out for the tell-tale powdery spots on the leaves. Gooseberries can also suffer from sawfly caterpillars stripping the leaves, but these are easily spotted and picked off.

KNOW-HOW

Gooseberries, redcurrants and white currants make attractive short standard trees that look great in pots, and they can also be trained on a wall or fence. Plant blackcurrant bushes about 5cm (2in) lower than they were previously planted to encourage stronger shoots to develop at the base.

RECOMMENDATIONS

Blackcurrant Ben Connan: a favourite of mine as it's such a prolific fruiter.

Blueberry Duke: fruits early, so great for areas with a short summer.

Gooseberry Pax: my choice for pain-free picking as it's almost spineless.

Redcurrant Red Lake: an old variety but one that stays popular due to its consistent fruiting and heavy crops of juicy fruit.

White Currant Blanka: huge crops of sweet, translucent fruits.

FRUIT TREES

Growing your own fruit trees is entirely possible in a small space. You might not have room for an orchard, but you will certainly have space for a trained tree or a miniature fruit tree grown in a pot.

CHOOSING
Fruit trees come on different sized rootstocks so make sure to buy a small or dwarf variety that will suit your space. Patio fruits are perfect for pots and espalier or fan-trained fruit trees can be pruned to fit their location.

PLANTING
The planting preparation is much the same for different types of fruit trees. If you're planting in the ground, remember these trees will be there a long time so make sure you give them the very best start you can. That means giving the ground a thorough dig, removing any weeds and adding in a good helping of well-rotted manure or garden compost to improve its drainage, structure and nutrient levels. Also choose your location carefully - all fruits need a good, sunny fence or wall to thrive, but for a peach to be really successful, it will need a sheltered south-facing wall.

Planting trees in containers means you can adjust the location more readily as they are portable, although if you go for a larger plant it will need a bigger container and might become a bit difficult to relocate. Soil also plays a huge part in the success of container-grown trees, so choose a soil-based compost such as John Innes No.3 for best results long term. This has more 'heart' than multi-purpose compost and will keep your tree happy for around five years, at which point you can re-pot the tree with some fresh John Innes No.3 to give it a boost.

WATERING AND FEEDING

If your trees are in pots then it's absolutely vital to water them well with a hose or large watering can most days during the growing season. This can take a while, so it might be worth buying an automatic system or making your own 'leaky hose'. Use an old length of hose pipe and make evenly spaced holes in one side of the pipe using a 0.5cm (¼in) drill bit. Add stop cap to the end and a tap fitting to the other end and lay the pipe close to the base of the plants you want to water.

A leaky hose (or seep hose) is often the best way to water trained trees planted in the ground. These won't need watering anywhere near as often as potted trees, but they will need some extra help during dry periods and when the fruit is developing.

Don't forget during the summer that even if it's rained you may still need to water by hand because the area of compost exposed to the rain is relatively small and the foliage canopy often stops most of the rain from penetrating. Plants and trees in pots also need more water because the compost heats up much more than the soil in the ground does.

TOP CHOICES FOR CONTAINERS

You can pick any variety of apples you fancy - as long as it's on a rootstock that will keep it nicely dwarfed. These will be clearly labelled or described as dwarf varieties. Ideally go for a self-fertile variety - otherwise you will need another tree to pollinate, which is the case with cooking apples such as Bramley's Seedling. My top choices include:

Red Falstaff: bright ruby red skin and sweet, crisp flesh.

Herefordshire Russet: classic 'nutty' russet flavour.

Saturn: disease resistant and a good all rounder.

When it comes to pear trees in pots, Concorde is the natural choice as it is compact, self-fertile and high yielding on even the smallest of trees.

Plums - and gages and damsons too, as they're all related - are great for pots when they're grafted onto the Pixy rootstock. Go for a classic Victoria plum or the earlier fruiting Opal, which is ready to pick in high summer.

Peaches and nectarines are a top choice for patio containers with their compact growth and lovely spring blossom. Added to that they almost always fruit in the first year after planting and they're also self-pollinating so you can have just a single tree. Top choices are Peregrine for its supersweet white flesh and Rochester with rich golden-fleshed fruits.

TOP CHOICES FOR TRAINING

For espaliers the best are always the spur-fruiting varieties that will produce reliable fruit year after year. Some top apple choices include:

Discovery: early fruiting old favourite with red fruits and a sharp flavour.

Greensleeves: an all-green variety with lovely fresh tasting fruit.

Sunset: reliable and late cropping.

Egremont Russet: the classic russet, reliable and good for storing.

Fiesta: easy and reliable as well as flavourful.

Top varieties of pears to grow include the well-established favourites

Conference: reliable and heavy cropping, even when grown on its own.

Doyenne du Comice: fabulous fruit, but needs a sunny spot.

For plums and peaches, the same varieties tend to be available as for containers except on larger growing rootstocks.

spring

summer, autumn

8 weeks

easy

full sun or
semi-shade

twice a week

0.6-1.8m (2-6ft)

yes

yes

fortnightly

BEANS

You may think that runner/string and French/green
beans are too big to grow in containers but many make
perfect crops to grow in pots. Dwarf varieties have been
specially developed for container growing, but even
some of the larger forms are brilliant for containers,
given enough space to grow and develop.

PLANTING

Start the seeds off indoors as they will germinate
quickly in the warm – they really don't like the cold.
Sow 2 seeds to a pot in spring about 3 weeks before
you want to plant outside, once the worst risk of frost
has passed.

GROWING

If you're growing the taller varieties, then a sheltered
spot is essential. You'll need a structure of bamboo
canes or a metal frame from the garden centre to
support these varieties. Once they're fully grown and
the masses of foliage is draping the supports, they can
be vulnerable to complete collapse in windy weather,
so make sure your supports are strong and sturdy. If
your location is very windy, you might be best going for
the bushy dwarf varieties. These are especially good
for tiny locations as they can grow happily in smaller
containers, even window boxes or troughs on a balcony.

Beans also need some sun each day, especially
French/green beans, although runner/string beans
are surprisingly shade tolerant and definitely the best
choice for a darker courtyard space.

Watering is critical, as it is with all container plants, but beans are especially thirsty when flowering. It's also worth spraying fully grown plants in flower and fruit with water when it's hot, to help with pollination.

HARVESTING

The crucial thing to do when harvesting beans is to keep on picking every 2-3 days. If you allow some of the beans to develop into big, gnarly pods, then the plant will stop flowering and producing more of those tender little beans.

PESKY PESTS

Once you get your newly planted beans beyond the keen attention of the slugs and snails, the main problem you'll encounter is the buds dropping or pods not setting, which is usually down to lack of watering. Occasionally you might spot aphids or red spider mite afflicting plants but usually this is when plants are stressed, again often due to poor watering.

KNOW-HOW

Runner/string beans originally come from Central America and grow all year round in their native warm, moist temperatures, whereas they get killed off by our autumnal frosts. Some varieties of runner bean date back to the 1850s, including the elegant and beautiful bi-colour Painted Lady.

RECOMMENDATIONS

Hestia: a bushy runner/string bean ideal for pots, with jazzy red and white flowers.

Sonesta: a dwarf French/green bean variety with colourful yellow pods.

Blue Lake: a classic, tall growing green podded French/green bean.

Red Rum: a super productive tall runner/string bean with jaunty red flowers.

CULINARY HERBS

A handful of herbs goes a long way in adding interest to your cooking and most of them are easy and attractive to grow in containers. Many Mediterranean herbs relish the warm, slightly dry conditions of container growing, but the downside is that they will often succumb during a cold wet winter, so many are best treated as a summer crop.

PLANTING
Sow seeds of annual herbs such as parsley, chervil and basil in pots indoors in spring. Annuals such as coriander/cilantro and dill are quick to grow and also quick to go to seed, so repeat sow a couple of pots frequently. Shrubby herbs like rosemary, thyme and sage are best bought as young plants from the garden centre in late spring and potted on, as are perennial favourites such as chives and French tarragon, although you could grow these from seed if you wish.

GROWING
All herbs need sunshine and, plenty of it, to thrive. Locate your pots in a sunny spot, ideally protected from frost, and raise them on pot feet or stones to aid drainage, as wet is the enemy of most herbs. You can make an attractive mixed pot of herbs or group them together.

○ spring, summer

❀ late spring, summer, autumn

▦ 4-6 weeks

▽ easy

☀ full sun or semi-shade

◁ weekly

↑↑ 45cm (18in)

❀ yes

◑ yes

◉ feed regularly

Many perennials like rosemary, bay and sage can be left in pots for several years before they need re-potting. Others such as mint are best grown on their own in a large pot, as they struggle with the confinement and become sparse and straggly. Mint particularly needs to be replanted every year using a generous portion of the root and a rich potting compost.

HARVESTING

Some herbs, such as mint, chives and French tarragon, die back naturally in the winter so harvest and dry them in late summer. Evergreens like rosemary and bay are pickable all through the winter, while thyme and sage often become a little sparse and may die off if the winter and their location is particularly wet and cold, so it's best to harvest and dry some leaves to be sure.

PESKY PESTS

Remarkably untroubled by pests, herbs mainly suffer from cold and wet, so location is crucial. Pick a spot where they won't be frosted, such as in the shelter of a wall or fence. Keep the worst of the rain off with a 'roof' of plywood if it's especially wet, and protect pots from freezing with bubble wrap or fleece if there is a very cold snap.

KNOW-HOW

Many pungent herbs are natural insect repellents so a well-placed vase of mixed herbs such as basil, mint, rosemary and lavender will help to deter flies and mosquitoes.

RECOMMENDATIONS

Basil Genovese: the classic lush and leafy Italian basil.

Thyme broad leaf: the hardiest variety I have grown with large, aromatic leaves.

Chives: so easy to grow, tasty and its pink flowers are attractive too, especially to bees.

Rosemary: a must-have herb for flavour, flower and it looks good in a pot.

ROOTS IN POTS

Growing your own root vegetables might seem out of the question if you're restricted to pots but actually many of these vegetables are surprisingly good in containers. Carrots, beetroot/beet and many other roots make great baby vegetable crops. Not only are they easy to keep an eye on and to protect from slugs and snails and other pests, but also the roots develop nicely in the softer medium of the compost, making for attractive and swift cropping.

PLANTING
Sow beetroot/beet in spring at 5cm (2in) apart and repeat sow into fresh containers at regular intervals. Carrots, too, can be sown from spring onwards at intervals but they have fine seed and will probably need thinning to 5cm (2in) apart.

GROWING
Don't use too rich a compost for growing roots or it can cause them to fork. A light, sandy compost such as John Innes No 3 is ideal. Thin as the plants develop, eating the thinnings as you go. Carrots will gradually need thinning to 7.5cm (3in) apart; beets to a little less, depending on the finished size you want your vegetables to be. Cover the carrot seedlings from late spring onwards with fleece to deter carrot root fly. Keep them watered and feed regularly.

💧	spring, summer
🌿	late spring, summer, autumn
📅	6 weeks
🪴	intermediate
☀️	full sun or semi-shade
💦	twice a week
↕️	30cm (12in)
🔋	feed regularly

HARVESTING

Harvest beetroot/beet leaves for salads frequently, pulling the roots once they're golf-ball size for the sweetest flavour. Carrots can be pulled once they're mature, although I always carry out gradual thinning, leaving them a little closer for a while and simply pulling the baby carrots for salads as I need to give the remaining plants more space.

PESKY PESTS

Slugs are the main problem around young seedlings so make the most of beer traps, sawdust or eggshell barriers (see pages 24-25). Avoid the attentions of carrot root fly by thinning seedlings in the evening and by covering containers with fleece.

KNOW-HOW

Beets are incredibly high in antioxidants, in fact just half a beetroot a day will give you all the antioxidants and nitrates your body needs.

RECOMMENDATIONS

Parmex: a lovely round carrot variety that's perfect for shallow containers.

Adelaide: early to mature, short-rooted carrots only 10cm (4in) long.

Pablo: a small, beautifully formed beetroot/beet that's great as a 'baby' or if left to mature.

Chioggia: an early maturing beetroot/beet with beautiful red and white striped roots.

spring, summer

summer, autumn

6-8 weeks

easy

full sun or semi-shade

daily or twice a week

20cm (8in)

SALADS IN CONTAINERS

Lettuces and their like are notoriously bad keepers, so what could be better than having some leafy salads at hand. Easy picking, cut-and-come-again salads grow like lightning and there are few things better than freshly harvested salad leaves in the height of summer. Add something special by sowing a few peas in a separate container to pick for tasty pea shoots.

PLANTING
Grow salads in troughs, window boxes, pots or grow bags – whatever comes to hand; just be ready to water regularly. Any container will do as long as it's at least 15cm (6in) deep and has good drainage.

Sow a ready-made salad mixture or single varieties – cut-and-come-again types will give you the best cropping in a small space. Sow thinly in late spring about 1–2cm ($\frac{1}{2}$–1in) apart after risk of frost has passed. For peas, choose a deeper container and sow the seeds about 5cm (2in) apart and 2cm (1in) deep.

GROWING
Keep the surface of the container moist by watering with a fine spray or rose on the watering can, but once the seedlings are up and growing strongly, water the compost directly and thoroughly.

HARVESTING

Harvesting can start as soon as the plants are 8-10cm (3-4in) tall. Pick a few leaves at a time or snip across the whole clump with scissors about 2.5cm (1in) above the ground. Keep on watering and these plants should regrow a couple more times.

Let the pea plants grow to 20cm (8in) tall before harvesting the top 5cm (2in) of the shoots. They will take a couple of weeks to regrow sufficiently to harvest again.

PESKY PESTS

Salads are very prone to slugs and snails so protect them accordingly (see pages 24-25). Raising the containers and grow bags off the ground on a frame helps.

KNOW-HOW

Even a small 30cm (12in) pot can produce the same quantity of leaves as several bags of supermarket salad.

RECOMMENDATIONS

Pea Sugar Ann: quick growing and sweet dwarf variety.

Lettuce Lollo Rosso: the classic cut-and-come-again lettuce.

Lettuce Oakleaf: reliable cropper with attractive leaves.

Cut-and-come-again varieties: a diverse mix of salad leaves.

COURGETTE OR ZUCCHINI

With their lush, large leaves and boisterous growth, these may not seem the obvious choice for cropping in a small space but courgettes/zucchini are a must-have. This summer vegetable is simply so easy to grow and so rewarding in that it fruits readily and for a long stretch of the summer.

PLANTING

Courgettes/zucchini are super easy to grow from seed, but are best started off indoors with individual seeds in pots. Start them off in mid to late spring, sowing each large seed on its side about 1.5cm (½in) deep in a 7.5cm (3in) pot.

GROWING

Once the plants have hardened off (see page 19), plant them outdoors in early summer, allowing each plant plenty of room to grow. Plant no more than 2 plants in a grow bag or a single plant in a large pot, and keep plants well watered through the season as they are thirsty growers.

HARVESTING

Courgettes/zucchini fruit very readily and need regular picking to keep the fruit coming. Pick them when they're 10cm (4in) or so long as they can become tough and tasteless if any larger.

spring

summer, autumn, winter

8 weeks

easy

full sun

twice a week

45cm (18in)

yes

feed regularly

PESKY PESTS

Courgettes/zucchini suffer from few pests once past the seedling stage, but they are prone to powdery mildew, where the leaves have a grey dust covering them. This happens if watering is insufficient when the weather is dry, but don't be confused by the natural silver marbling on the leaves of some varieties. Plants can also suffer from poor fruiting, especially when the weather is cold, but this should improve as temperatures rise.

KNOW-HOW

Courgette/zucchini flowers are also edible and can be eaten raw in salads or stuffed and fried. Varieties with darker coloured fruit contain the greatest amounts of nutrients.

RECOMMENDATIONS

Defender: a deep green favourite which is a prolific fruiter.

Gold Rush: golden yellow fruits and plenty of them.

One Ball: small, perfectly round fruits.

EDIBLE FLOWERS

Many of these companion planting flowers are also edible, which adds a great deal of pizzazz to your salads and table settings. There's something special about a few brilliantly coloured flowers and petals scattered over a dish that makes even the simplest meal look amazing.

HERB FLOWERS
Many of the most common herbs such as rosemary, lavender and chives have flowers that are edible. You have to go easy with them though, as they can have a powerful taste.

Chives are one of my favourites – the flowers have a crunchy onion note to them, but you'll need to separate the florets otherwise they're too full-on. Chive flowers are great added to mashed potato, tomato salad or mixed with soft cheese instead of spring onion/scallion.

Sage, rosemary and thyme flowers are all good in salads or added as a garnish to soups, while the aniseed flavour of fresh, new fennel flowers is great with pork, fish and rice.

Lavender adds a wonderful fragrance to sweet things, but you have to be very spare using it in cooking or your finished dish will taste a bit like soap. The best trick is to use a couple of flower heads to flavour some sugar (just pop a couple of clean flower spikes in a jar of sugar and leave to infuse), then use that for sweetening cream or making cakes or shortbread. Pair it with lemon juice or zest for a winning combination.

EASY ANNUALS

There are so many of these quick-to-grow and quick-to-flower annuals that deserve a place in your tiny space for several reasons besides the fact they're edible. To name but a few, plants such as nasturtium, calendula, borage and viola are brilliant for bringing in essential bees and other insects to pollinate your vegetables and fruits, as well as brightening up the garden immeasurably.

Nasturtium flowers and young leaves add a delicious peppery flavour to salads, while calendula petals can be used in place of saffron to colour and flavour dishes like tagines.

Borage flowers have a cucumber freshness to them that is good in drinks and salads, while dainty violas have a subtle floral taste and look adorable as a garnish for cakes, desserts and salads.

VEGETABLE FLOWERS

Ask any Italian and they will tell you that courgette/zucchini flowers are almost as important a crop as the vegetable itself. These large golden flowers, and the ones from squash plants too, can be chopped into salads or, even better, stuffed with cream cheese and cooked. Only pick the male flowers on the long thin stalks - leave the female flowers to bear the fruit. Look behind the flower before you pick and you can see the tiny fruit developing.

Another Italian favourite are rocket/arugula flowers. Rocket has an annoying habit of bolting into flower very quickly and you can slow this down by removing all the flower stalks as they appear. Even better, eat the peppery yet sweet flowers in salads as you go.

EXTEND THE SEASON

Making the most of a small growing space means pushing the boundaries of the seasons. Usually, cold weather stops you planting early in the season and, likewise, autumnal frosts will put paid to the lush summer crops. However, there are some vegetables that will cope with the cold temperatures, many of them actually needing a cold period to stimulate them into growth. Protecting the crops means you can start growing earlier and finish cropping later. This will extend your growing season and you may be able to keep on harvesting throughout the winter months.

START EARLY

When it comes to growing outdoors, many crops such as carrots need a warm soil to get them germinating, but there are some crops that are happy to be started off early in colder soils. As a general rule these seem to be crops with a lot of reserves of nutrients and energy built in to the actual seed - broad/fava beans and early peas come to mind. These toughies will cope with inhospitable weather as they're planted deeper than small seeds (see page 131) and push off to a good start from those fleshy seeds.

Some of the best winter growers are actually those that you plant in late autumn or early winter for early harvesting the following spring. Overwintered garlic, broad/fava beans and peas all make some growth beneath the soil before winter, and accelerate into active growth as soon as the weather begins to warm up.

A LITTLE EXTRA PROTECTION

Given a heated propagator or a grow lamp, there are many seeds that you can get started early in the season. Plants like chillies, aubergines/eggplants and basil will all get off to a swift start and can be nurtured indoors for a few weeks while the ground is warming up outside.

Outdoor crops - even those fussy carrots - can also be sown early, provided they get a little extra protection in the form of fleece. Ideally warm the soil or pots for a few days before sowing by covering them with fleece, weighted down with stones or pegged down to keep it secure. Continue to keep them covered once you've sown the seeds, at least at night, while the weather is cold and especially so if frost is forecast.

FINISH LATE
There are some vegetables that are traditionally sown in spring, but are ready to harvest late, such as maincrop potatoes, squashes and pumpkins, which all come into their own in autumn. Add to those a mid to late season sowing of dependable crops that will see you well into the autumn and perhaps even early winter, if you have a sheltered spot or you use fleece to protect your crops. Think about making additional sowings of stalwarts such as beetroot/beets, carrots, kohl rabi and chard in high summer for cropping a few weeks or even months later.

WINTER PICKING
There are specific crops that you can sow in late summer that will 'stand' ready for picking as the winter unfolds. Winter-cropping varieties of cabbage and kale are especially robust for winter harvesting, but later sowings of many summertime crops like chard, turnips and winter salad mixes will also give plenty of picking.

GARLIC

Growing your own garlic is surprisingly easy, takes up less space than you might imagine and is by far the best garlic that you will ever eat. Don't be confused by the two types available – the easiest type is the softneck, which also stores very well. Hardneck garlic is purported to have the better flavour but in general it doesn't store and is less tough.

PLANTING
Ideally, plant garlic in the late autumn, splitting the bulbs carefully and planting single cloves 15cm (6in) apart at twice their own depth. You can also plant in spring, but the harvest will be later in summer and the bulbs won't be anything like as large.

GROWING
Garlic really is no trouble to grow. Keep the plants weeded and watered, removing any flower buds as they develop (these 'scapes' are delicious added to stir-fries).

HARVESTING
Harvest once the leaves start to turn yellow, digging the bulbs up with a trowel and laying them to dry off for a day or so in a sunny spot. Store them by plaiting the bulbs together, bunching them or laying them individually in a tray.

 autumn, spring

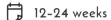 summer

12-24 weeks

 easy

full sun or semi-shade

weekly

45cm (18in)

PESKY PESTS

Rust – a fungal problem causing little rusty blotches on the leaves – is likely to be the worst problem your garlic will encounter. It's more prevalent in wet weather on plants that are mature, and the bulbs are best harvested swiftly once it's spotted.

KNOW-HOW

You can plant supermarket garlic cloves, but the chances are your crop will not be as good as if you planted specially grown planting garlic from a seed supplier or garden centre. These bulbs are specially treated to be virus free and they're also varieties that have been developed to cope with the regional climate.

RECOMMENDATIONS

Chesnok Red: a hardy hardneck variety with a super flavour.

Solent Wight: reliable softneck which is a brilliant keeper.

Thermidrome: mild softneck variety.

BROAD, FAVA OR FABA BEANS

These easy-to-grow, pretty beans are one of the first crops to be ready for harvesting and taste super sweet when they're young and fresh.

PLANTING

In a sheltered garden, planting broad/fava or faba beans in early winter means they germinate and grow a little before winter stops them. The beans then get off to a racing start as soon as spring starts and they'll be ready for picking by late spring. Planting in late winter and early spring isn't quite as swift, but does still give early crops.

Plant densely about 15-20cm (6-9in) apart and sow a few extra plants in pots in case you need to fill in any gaps.

GROWING

In cold winter weather, use a cloche or drape of fleece to protect your overwintering beans. Don't forget to water them if the weather is dry – winter winds can be especially drying.

Once the lowest flowers have started to form small pods, pinch out the tips of the plant to encourage bushiness and to help stop blackfly getting a hold. You can eat those tips in a stir-fry.

late autumn, late winter, spring

late spring, summer

15–25 weeks

easy

full sun or semi-shade

weekly

60cm (24in)

yes

HARVESTING

You can eat the pods whole when they are very young, but for the beans themselves it's a wait for the pods to swell significantly. Small and sweet is how you really want to eat your beans, so pick regularly, starting from the bottom of the plant.

PESKY PESTS

Beans are surprisingly robust. The worst problem you're likely to see is a lack of germination due to mice eating the beans – that's when those spare plants come in handy. Also, blackfly is a real pest but it's less prevalent early in the season, so the earlier your beans are ready for cropping the better. That makes sowing them in the autumn even more of a good idea.

KNOW-HOW

All beans and legumes are incredibly useful for fixing essential nitrogen in the soil, as they form nodules on their roots where nitrogen becomes stored as they grow. Broad/fava beans are no exception. They're also especially useful as a cover crop for fallow beds – those you're not using for a while – especially if your garden is windy, as they will help to protect and secure the soil from eroding.

RECOMMENDATIONS

Aquadulce Claudia: the go-to variety for autumn planting.

The Sutton: a good dwarf choice for the containers and beds.

Stereo: less hardy but great for eating whole.

Crimson Flowered: beautiful but only for spring sowing.

KALE

Hardy and resilient, kale will just keep on growing, giving you leafy greens all through winter.

PLANTING
Sow seeds between spring and summer in a seedbed or pots and thin to 7.5cm (3in) apart or a single plant per pot. You can eat the thinnings as salad leaves.

GROWING
Transplant from the seedbed or pots once the plants have at least 5-6 strong leaves. Plant them deeply about 40cm (16in) apart or in large individual pots, with the lowest leaves brushing the ground. Water them well before and after you transplant.

HARVESTING
Start picking hand-sized leaves from the bottom of the plant in autumn. Pick a handful of leaves from each plant at one time and avoid harvesting the top shoot until you're ready to replace the plant.

PESKY PESTS
It's essential to cover the crop with netting or fleece throughout its growing season to deter birds. If you spot caterpillars of cabbage white butterflies in the summer, simply pick them off or use a fine-gauge netting to stop the butterflies laying their eggs in the first place.

KNOW-HOW
After the top of the plant is harvested, side shoots may form and give you a last crop of tender leaf shoots.

spring, summer

autumn, winter, early spring

8-10 weeks

easy

full sun or semi-shade

weekly

60cm (24in)

TOP CHOICES
Cavolo Nero: the classic black Tuscan kale so beloved of chefs.

Redbor: richly coloured red-purple leaves that look very attractive in the garden as well as tasting good.

Kapitan: a dwarf, deep green variety with densely curled leaves.

💧	spring
🌿	autumn
📅	12-16 weeks
🪣	easy
☀️	full sun or semi-shade
💦	weekly
🌱	90cm (3ft) but trail to 4m (12ft)
🌰	yes but sometimes not viable

PUMPKIN AND SQUASHES

Although these are a long-term crop, growing throughout the summer, they're great to fit into an odd spot, very fruitful late in the season and store well.

PLANTING
Sow 2 seeds in individual pots in late spring indoors to get them off to a good start. Don't sow too many – a couple of pots will be plenty – and place the flat seeds sideways into the compost 1.5cm (½in) deep. Once they germinate, thin to the strongest seedling and grow on to a good size before planting out in early summer.

You can sow outdoors in late spring once the risk of frost is over but, in my experience, it's not as successful as sowing indoors.

GROWING
Pumpkins and squashes might start off small but they do take up a lot of space once they really get growing. Plant them in large pots, grow bags, raised beds or even a corner of the compost heap. They're trailing plants so you can encourage the stems up fences and walls or allow them to sprawl along paths. Take care they don't swamp other plants though.

HARVESTING
Summer squashes are more like courgettes/zucchini and need picking regularly, while the winter squashes and pumpkins should be left to swell and ripen all

through the summer. Raise the fruits off the ground on a piece of wood or a tile and leave the fruit to ripen on the plant until the weather starts to decline in the autumn. Harvest before the frost strikes.

PESKY PESTS

The worst problem is slugs and snails on initial planting out, so protect each plant with a barrier of grit or beer traps (see pages 24-25). As the plants grow, good watering is essential - watch out for powdery splotches on the leaves which indicate the plant is becoming too dry.

KNOW-HOW

Pumpkin and squash flowers are also edible and pumpkin seeds are known to have medicinal properties and are rich in nutrients, vitamins and unsaturated fats. They're especially good for your heart, cholesterol and blood sugar levels and may be helpful in reducing the risk of cancer.

RECOMMENDATIONS

Harrier: a butternut squash that's been specially bred for cool climates.

Uchiki Kuri: my favourite Kabocha squash has bright orange skin and flesh and is marvellous for storing.

Turk's Turban: fabulously ornamental and great to eat, too.

Pumpkin Baby Bear: small, perfect pumpkins that are great to eat - even the seeds.

WINTER GREENS

Summer leaves such as chard, chicory or radicchio, rocket/arugula and even herbs like parsley and chervil can keep on cropping into winter with a little added protection from fleece or cloches.

PLANTING
Sow these crops as soon as you can in spring to get leaves early in the summer but, for overwintering, it's wise to sow a second burst in summer. This gives these new plants a good chance to grow and bulk up so they're in their prime in the autumn, whereas the older plants will be past their best.

GROWING
Make the most of your available space by planting these crops in the gaps, pots and spaces left by early crops such as broad/fava beans and early potatoes.

Make sure to keep the plants well watered during the summer season while they're establishing and cover them with cloches or fleece once the temperatures start to dip.

HARVESTING
Picking little and often is the best policy so the plants don't become too stressed. Take a few snippings of leaves at a time, allowing some leaves to remain so the plant will keep on growing.

- spring, summer
- autumn, winter
- 8 weeks
- intermediate
- full sun or semi-shade
- weekly
- 60cm (24in)

PESKY PESTS

Leafy crops are prone to bolting if they become stressed so keep them sheltered and moist, but not too wet. Protect the leaves from pigeons with netting if you aren't using fleece or cloches and watch out for slugs and snails, as always.

KNOW-HOW

Many summer crops will overwinter successfully for smaller harvest but they will start to bolt and flower as soon as the days lengthen in the spring.

RECOMMENDATIONS

Rocket/Arugula Astra: quick growing, peppery and slow to bolt.

Radicchio Rossa di Treviso: colourful and incredibly hardy.

Chard Bright Lights: brilliantly colourful stems and leafy tops.

EAT THE UNUSUAL

Just because your space is small it doesn't mean you can't have some fun with it. Growing a few unusual crops adds a touch of adventure to your season and these crops aren't the sorts of thing you'll find in the shops either. I wouldn't necessarily devote a huge area to them - you don't know if you're going to like the taste of them after all - but there is a wide choice of unusual and fun plants to grow. These aren't your staple crops but they do add a sense of fun and variety, so why not grow a different one or two each season.

- 💧 spring
- 🌿 summer
- 📅 10 weeks
- 🪣 easy
- ☀️ full sun
- 💧 twice a week or more
- ⬆️ 90cm (3ft)
- ❀ yes
- 🌱 yes
- 🌼 weekly

CUCAMELONS

These tiny striped and speckled fruits are easy to grow and taste like a cucumber and lime combined. These 'mouse melons', as they are known in Mexico, are also drought tolerant and just one plant goes a long way.

PLANTING
Sow seeds in spring into individual pots 1cm (½in) deep and keep them cosy in a propagator on the windowsill.

GROWING
Grow cucamelons outdoors in a warm, sunny spot, either in the border, in a grow bag or a large pot. Space plants 30cm (12in) apart, provide them with a cane for support and water and feed regularly. Pinch out the main growing shoot once it is 2.5m (8ft) tall, as well as any side shoots once they are 40cm (16in) or so.

HARVESTING
Pick the fruits once they're the size of olives and use them in salads, pickle them whole or serve them with drinks. You can also use them for salsa.

PESKY PESTS
Pests aren't usually a problem, but do pick regularly or the fruits will become soft and bitter and stop forming.

KNOW-HOW
You can overwinter the cucamelon plant by cutting it back in the autumn and storing the root in compost in the shed before planting it out again in spring.

ASPARAGUS PEAS

These attractive winged peapods have the look of okra but a hint of asparagus flavour. Easy to grow, asparagus peas also make a pretty addition to the garden with their deep red flowers.

PLANTING
Sow seeds in spring into individual pots, preferably indoors or you can sow directly outside in warmer weather. The seedlings should appear in a week or so.

GROWING
Plant out in a sunny spot once any risk of frost is gone, setting plants 10cm (4in) apart. Grow them in the border, raised bed, in grow bags or pots.

HARVESTING
Pick the pods when they're no longer than 2.5cm (1in) - think of them as baby mange tout peas - otherwise the pods become tough. Cook them whole, steaming lightly, and serve with a pat of butter.

PESKY PESTS
Pests aren't usually a problem, but good watering when they're flowering and producing pods is crucial.

KNOW-HOW
Records of growing asparagus peas date back to the 1600s and they can be found growing throughout the Mediterranean region, Europe and Asia.

 spring

summer, autumn

7 weeks

easy

full sun

weekly

60cm (24in)

yes

yes

feed regularly once flowering

TOMATILLO

Tomatillos are a Mexican favourite that look like a cross between a tomato and a cape gooseberry and make amazing salsas with their tart, 'green grape' flavour.

PLANTING
Sow seeds in spring into individual pots in a propagator on the windowsill. Germination should take about 10 days. Grow at least two plants to allow for pollination.

GROWING
Grow tomatillos outdoors in a warm, sunny spot, either in the border, in a grow bag or a large pot, planting the stems deeply and staking them sturdily. Although these plants are more drought tolerant than tomatoes, it's a good idea to feed and water the plants regularly.

HARVESTING
Pick the fruits once they're bright green and filling out the papery husks. Once they break the husk and turn yellow or purple, they're over-ripe. You can store green tomatillos in their husks in the fridge for 2-3 weeks.

PESKY PESTS
Pests aren't usually a problem.

KNOW-HOW
The tomatillo has been grown as a food crop in South America for millennia and was domesticated in about 800 BCE by the Aztecs. It seeds itself freely and is something of a weed in some USA regions.

 spring

summer, autumn

10-14 weeks

intermediate

full sun

weekly

60cm (24in)

yes

yes

feed regularly

- spring, summer
- summer, autumn
- 6 weeks
- easy
- full sun
- weekly
- 60cm (24in)
- yes
- yes

AMARANTH OR CALLALOO

Amaranth has a great many names depending on where in the world you are. All varieties are edible and you can eat both the leaves and the seeds.

PLANTING
Sow the fine seeds in spring in a propagator or directly into the ground once warmer outside. The seeds should take about 10 days to germinate.

GROWING
Grow amaranth in a sunny, warm spot ideally, although the plants are very tolerant of less than ideal conditions.

HARVESTING
Much like spinach, pick the leaves when you need and steam, stir-fry them or use young leaves fresh in salads.

PESKY PESTS
Slugs and snails are a problem as the seeds germinate and grow, but after this stage, there is little trouble.

KNOW-HOW
Recently, amaranth has been grown for its flowers – not just food – particularly the form 'Love Lies Bleeding'.

RECOMMENDATIONS
Hopi Red Dye: deep red leaves with tasselled flowers.

Amaranthus Tricolor or Joseph's Coat: splashed foliage or green, red and gold on bushy plants.

MUSHROOMS

Growing your own mushrooms isn't easy if you try to do the process yourself – it's far simpler to buy a kit.

PLANTING
Traditionally mushrooms are grown on sterilized straw in a closely controlled environment. Using a mushroom kit or specially prepared log is easier but good hygiene and even temperatures are still needed for success.

GROWING
Grow button or chestnut mushrooms in a compost-based kit, or shiitake mushrooms on a log, while oyster mushrooms usually come in a treated straw kit. All will need to be kept moist by spraying the surface with water once or twice a day. Keep your kit out of direct sunlight with an even temperature of 18°C (65°F).

HARVESTING
Harvest button and chestnut mushrooms by twisting the fungi, removing the whole root. These should fruit within 3 weeks. Shiitake and oyster mushrooms can be as quick as 7 days from a kit.

PESKY PESTS
Pests aren't usually a problem, but lack of humidity is the biggest issue and will lead to poor cropping.

KNOW-HOW
Estimated to be more than 8,000 years old, the largest living organism on the planet is a fungus that covers almost 40km^2 (15mi^2) of forest in Oregon, USA.

spring, summer

spring, summer, autumn, winter

1-3 weeks

challenging

full or semi-shade

twice a day

60cm (24in)

LEMONS

A lemon tree won't give you enough lemons to make lemonade, but it will give you a great deal of satisfaction and joy.

PLANTING
Lemon trees make wonderful potted trees, growing 1-1.5m (3-5ft) in height, although you can get taller varieties if you wish. The beautifully fragrant flowers appear in spring and the fruit ripens on average 12 months later, which means they're often in flower and fruit at the same time. You can grow lemon trees from pips or cuttings, but many bought trees are grafted onto dwarf rootstocks to keep them small enough to move indoors and out easily.

GROWING
Lemon trees are the hardiest of the citrus fruits, but they will still need to be kept indoors in the winter months, either in a porch, a cool room or a heated greenhouse. In summer, they love being in a sunny sheltered spot outdoors. They need regular feeding and watering throughout the summer months but should be kept on the dry side in winter.

HARVESTING
Pick the fruit as it ripens but don't be afraid to keep the fruit on the tree until you need it.

PESKY PETS
The main pests are indoor ones. These usually lessen once the plant is outside for the summer and predators such as ladybirds/ladybugs can get to them.

spring, summer

spring, summer, autumn, winter

40-52 weeks

challenging

full sun or semi-shade

twice a week in summer, once or twice a week in winter

0.6-1.8m (2-6ft)

TOP CHOICES
Eureka: lush foliage and plenty of fruit.

Four Seasons: good, reliable fruiter.

Dwarf varieties: produce the most lemons per size of tree.

GARDENERS' DICTIONARY

BOLTING
This is when a plant stops growing in its normal way and sends up a flowering shoot. It usually happens when a plant is stressed due to lack of water or something similar, or when it's towards the end of its cropping life.

CHITTING
Some varieties of potato are 'chitted' to get them growing before they're planted out. This means placing the potato in a light spot to encourage the 'eyes' or tiny buds on the potato to sprout.

CLOCHE
A covering of glass or plastic, which acts as a miniature greenhouse for keeping the plants warm and safe from frost early in the season.

FALLOW
Leaving a bed to lie 'fallow' simply means leaving it unplanted for a while. It's mostly done to rest the bed and allow weeds to grow so you can clear them before planting.

FLEECE
Horticultural fleece is a woven fabric that can be pinned down to warm the soil before planting and keep seedlings warm as they emerge and develop. It's also useful for wrapping larger, tender plants in cold weather to protect them from wind and frost.

PINCHING OUT
Using your fingers to nip off the tips of shoots to encourage branching or to 'stop' a trailing plant such as pumpkin from growing any longer. This encourages the plant to focus its energies on producing fruit rather than simply growing.

POTTING ON
After you have 'pricked out' (see overleaf) your seedlings, they will need potting on into pots to grow on some more before planting out.

PRICKING OUT

This is the delicate job of separating seedlings grown en masse in a seed tray into individual plants for potting on. Use a pencil or a plant label to gently separate the seedlings, holding them only by their tiny seed leaves and supporting their fragile roots with your pencil or label to move them to their allotted pot.

SEED LEAVES

The first leaves a seedling produces are a simple pair of leaves which are then followed by the 'true' leaves - the leaves that look like the mature plant.

THINNING

Removing some young plants from an area or row to allow others to develop fully. Fruit on fruit trees such as apples and pears are also 'thinned' at a young stage to allow the remaining fruits to grow larger and have good air circulation around them.

CORDON

A fruit tree that is trained flat against a wall as a single main stem, often grown at a 45-degree angle.

ESPALIER

A fruit tree that is trained flat against a wall, fence or wires in a series of tiered branches.

HARDENING OFF

The process of gradually acclimatizing tender plants and seedlings to the outdoors in readiness for planting them out. These plants have been started off indoors or in a greenhouse and are accustomed to steady, warm temperatures so they need a period of gentle adjustment, otherwise the sudden shock of cool winter nights might kill them off.

DAMPING OFF

A disease that seedlings are prone to in the early stages just before or just after germination. Improved by sowing thinly, careful watering and good ventilation.

ROOTSTOCK

Fruit trees - and other plants - are often grown on a different rootstock to manage their growth so their final size is predictable. Rootstocks often also give the plant improved vigour and health.

ACKNOWLEDGEMENTS

Huge thanks to Emli Bendixen whose brilliant pictures give life and substance to my words.

My thanks also go to Harriet Butt, Alicia House and the rest of the Quadrille team and to Jane Graham Maw and Maddy Belton for being so supportive.

The biggest thanks of all must go to my friend Anna and my partner Paul, who both put up with me going on about fruit and vegetables rather a lot.

MANAGING DIRECTOR
Sarah Lavelle
SENIOR COMMISSIONING EDITOR
Harriet Butt
ASSISTANT EDITOR Oreolu Grillo
SERIES DESIGNER Gemma Hayden
DESIGNER Alicia House
PHOTOGRAPHER Emli Bendixen
HEAD OF PRODUCTION
Stephen Lang
PRODUCTION CONTROLLER
Sabeena Atchia

Published in 2021 by Quadrille,
an imprint of Hardie Grant Publishing

Quadrille
52-54 Southwark Street
London SE1 1UN
quadrille.com

Cataloguing in Publication Data:
a catalogue record for this book
is available from the British Library.

Text © Jane Moore 2021
Photography © Emli Bendixen 2021
Design and layout © Quadrille 2021

ISBN 978 1 78713 731 8
Printed in China

FSC
www.fsc.org

MIX
Paper from
responsible sources
FSC™ C020056